KU-789-970

The Americanization of the Global Village:
Essays in Comparative Popular Culture

Edited by Roger Rollin

Bowling Green State University Popular Press
Bowling Green, Ohio 43403

Copyright © 1989 by Bowling Green State University Popular Press

Library of Congress Catalogue Card No.: 89-083393

ISBN: 0-87972-469-2 Clothbound
      0-87972-470-6 Paperback

Cover design by Gregg Budgett and Gary Dumm

Dedicated with love and respect to
the winner of the 1984 Whatley Award
for the best essay in *Studies in Popular Culture* that year,
my wife, Lucy Rollin

Contents

Introduction
On Comparative Popular Culture, American Style

Roger Rollin

The American Hamburger in the Global Village:
A Personal Perspective

In the mid-Fifties I was in the U.S. Army, stationed in Austria and Germany. There, where "hamburger" was invented, the only place you could get *a* hamburger was a military establishment—a PX or an Army or Air Force Club. I can't be sure, but I suspect they imported the ingredients from the States, as they did a lot of what we ate. It was as if the genuine article, real American-type food, couldn't be made from "foreign" ingredients.

In the mid-Sixties I was on sabbatical leave in England. You *could* get a "hamburger" in England then, at a chain restaurant called "Wimpey's." My children, aged eleven and eight, would beg to stop at Wimpey's for a "hamburger" when we traveled—but they were attending English schools, eating English school lunches, and actually enjoying food with names like "Shepherd's Pie" and "Bubble and Squeak." My wife and I, however, knew that if a Wimpey-burger actually began to taste like a hamburger to you, you'd been in England too long.

Recently I was back in England for a vacation. In Oxford alone there seemed to be a McDonald's on every other block, not to mention Kentucky Fried Chicken and Pizza Hut. You could walk into these establishments and almost feel as if you were in Dubuque. Today, of course, you can do just about the same in Tokyo and Hamburg and even in the capital of *haute cuisine*, Paris. The world has been McDonaldized.

"Is this progress?" asks the cynic. The question, however, is out of order. "Progress," like beauty, is finally in the eye of the beholder, more a matter of taste or opinion than a matter of fact. A more pertinent question might be, "What effects has the McDonaldizing of other countries had upon their food industries and national nutrition-level,

1

and upon the eating habits and the food attitudes, beliefs, and values of their peoples?"

To put it more generally, to what extent has the Americanizing of the global village changed the lives, including the hearts and minds, of the inhabitants of that village? It is an important question, though often, it seems, more important to those on the receiving end of American exports than to most Americans. Comparative popular culture studies can begin to answer this question because so much of that Americanization-process is carried out through our mass media and their chief product, American popular culture. And begin it must. Otherwise we have only the mainly personal (and seldom unbiased) impressions foisted upon us by politicians, journalists, and ordinary travelers. And the precarious stability and harmony of the global village are too important to Americans and everyone else for it to be left to that.

America in the Eyes of the Global Village: An Anecdote

Back in the early Sixties, we invited a Nigerian college student to have Christmas dinner with us. During the tabletalk I asked him, "What about the United States turned out to be most different from your expectations after you had arrived here?" Our intelligent and sophisticated guest thought for a moment and then, in his distinctively Anglo-African dialect, said quite seriously, "I had expected there would be more of a cowboy problem."

Another question, then, that comparative popular culture studies can usefully address is, "What impressions of the United States have been and are being created by the Americanization of the global village?" While not all of this Americanizing is being done by means of popular culture, of course, a great deal of it is. And while eating a Big Mac may have no more significant an impact upon the lifestyle and culture of a Londoner or a Parisian than dining on fish and chips or croissants will affect a Chicagoan, what the rest of the world thinks it knows about the United States, its history, its policies, its people, its beliefs and values and lifestyles, comes mainly from the mass media—chiefly television, movies, music, and popular books and magazines. Such impressions, it is reasonable to assume, can affect how citizens of other lands spend their leisure time, make purchases, set personal goals, perceive the world, and even vote.

The State of Comparative Popular Culture Studies:
An Impression

Scholarship has this much at least in common with the world of business: sometimes things get done only because someone identifies a need that is not being met, and by meeting that need gains a reputation and rewards from the less insightful. This is as true of the development of popular culture studies as it is of McDonald's. Like Ray Kroc, academics such as Ray Browne, Russell Nye, Carl Bode, and Marshall Fishwick recognized the need for something new: a fresh, scholarly approach to what other intellectuals had for so long been dismissing as mere *kitsch*, "lowbrow" or "sub-" "culture." That is, these American originators of the popular culture studies movement recognized the need for a serious investigation of what millions of quite responsible human beings found gratifying enough to spend much of their leisure time, energy, and disposable income upon—movies, television, popular music, sports, popular magazines and books, etc.

The academic community gradually came to acknowledge that there was indeed important work to be done. Nevertheless, it was apparent that the number of scholars willing and able to explore this new field without benefit of the usual scholarly insurance, though growing, was limited. Decisions had to be made about what specific topics seemed to be manageable as well as interesting and important. Moreover, the absence of an extensive body of previous scholarship meant that, along with one's specific research, one had to develop some kind of working definition or theory of popular culture so as to be able to contextualize one's thinking. And develop appropriate and effective methodologies as well. Since formal popular culture study is less than a few decades old, then, it is not surprising that the body of knowledge it has amassed contains a variety of *lacunae*. One of the more significant of these is comparative popular culture studies.

The first and still the primary source of scholarship in popular culture, the *Journal of Popular Culture*, has from its beginnings attempted to be international in scope. That is, it has regularly published articles on the popular culture of other countries and frequently featured "in-depth" sections on the popular culture of a particular region or nation— for example, Canada (14:2), Latin America (14:3), Japan (17:1), Bulgaria (19:1), and Colombia (22:1). But if, by comparative popular culture, we mean scholarship that makes a deliberate effort to compare and contrast the culture consumed by masses of people in two different countries or world regions, relatively few published popular culture articles and books fit the definition. The essays in this book, to varying degrees (inevitably), do. Moreover, all of them attempt to compare and contrast aspects of the popular culture of the United States with that of other countries—appropriate since the United States is the world's largest producer and most successful exporter of popular culture.

Most of the essays that follow were first delivered as papers given in two sessions sponsored by the Modern Language Association's Popular Culture Division at the 1987 MLA meeting. Why they are among the relatively few examples of comparative popular culture scholarship extant and what may be done to improve this situation bear brief examination.

The fact that, for many of the years since the end of World War II, the United States has had a positive balance of payments may have something to do with the benign neglect of comparative popular culture. So long as the U.S. was the world's largest exporter of cultural as well as many other products, there was far more concern abroad about the impact of American popular culture on other peoples than there was at home (for two cases in point, see Chantal Cinquin's "President Mitterand Also Watches *Dallas*" and "Images of the United States in Selected Mexican Comic Books" by Charles Tatum.) Such expressions of alarm concerning the possible influence of U.S. movies, television, music, and popular journalism were easily dismissed as manifestations of anti-American hysteria: Mickey Mouse Go Home! Besides, it could be difficult for Americans to see much wrong with exporting entertainment: that was, after all, the American Way—and, at that, a way of promulgating the American Way in areas that (some felt) could probably do with a bit of it. The fact that Americans as a whole experienced little sense of urgency about the exportation of their popular culture and its ramifications, then, may have contributed to the American academy's neglect of comparative popular culture scholarship.

But when the balance of payments began to shift against the U.S., even though popular (or any other kind) of foreign culture had relatively little to do with that shift, it became easier to empathize with the "invasion mentality" of other peoples. That is, as, first, the Beetle, then the Beatles, and then the Sonys began to loom larger and larger in the American lifestyle, it became somewhat easier for U.S. citizens to appreciate the sense of many in other countries that their national identity, their culture, their lifestyle, even their consciousness, were being invaded (an act perceivable only as aggression) by foreigners. Obviously, there is a qualitative difference between buying a Honda and watching a dubbed version of *Dallas,* but some element of disjunction or displacement seems inevitable in both experiences. Living as they do, not in ivory towers, but in the real world of car payments and mortgages, scholars are also susceptible to such feelings. And scholars, being scholars, are inclined to ask themselves *why* the consumption of foreign products should generate emotions of disjunction and displacement.

By the late Seventies and the early Eighties it was becoming possible for even the ordinary citizen to begin to worry about, first, "the Arabs taking over this country," and then, the Japanese and the Koreans. Since then, it has become increasingly possible to recognize that the importance of comparative popular culture studies resides, not only in the impact of American popular culture abroad, but also in the effects of the influx of foreign peoples, their cultures, and their products into the United States. Although the feature film, *Gung Ho!*, dealing with a Japanese takeover of an American factory, was scarcely a blockbuster, and the television series based upon it was short-lived, these are not likely to be the last comic (or serious) attempts to address pertinent cross-cultural issues for a mass audience. Such creative efforts need to be examined as potential barometers of the American mass audience's perceptions of and attitudes towards the rest of the global village.

Humanities scholars are not the only ones who have tended to overlook the area of popular culture or to underestimate its importance. Although social anthropologists and other social scientists with an interest in acculturation have done considerable research into intercultural phenomena, they do not always pay much attention to the predominant mode of acculturation today, the mass media, or to the latters' main product, popular culture. For example, in all the 221 pages of UNESCO'S publication, *Introduction to Intercultural Studies* (Paris: UNESCO, 1983), there are little more than half a dozen references— and these mainly in passing—to the mass media, mass culture, or popular culture. The international conference that gave rise to this volume focused its attention far more on such issues as culture theory, language and cultural identity than to such specific matters as how much actual importation of films, TV, popular music, popular magazines and books actually goes on, world-wide, or how and for what purposes such culture materials are being "consumed" by their users.

Another reason for the paucity of comparative popular culture studies published up to now has probably been a kind of accident of history: most of the founding fathers of the popular culture movement in the United States came from the fields of English or American Studies, as did those who followed them, the second generation of popular culture scholars. For some reason foreign language and comparative literature scholars have been somewhat slow to become involved in the new field. And yet it is, of course, foreign language and comparative literature scholars who typically will be best qualified to engage in comparative popular culture studies. Their formal training has given them the sophisticated linguistic skills so essential to such scholarship. Moreover, their study—and often their experience—of life in another society enable them to transcend their own ethnocentricity to a greater extent than can the average American humanist or social scientist. It is no coincidence that, of the nine essays which follow, all but two of them were written by foreign language or comparative literature specialists.

Similar Issues, Different Approaches, Compatible Conclusions
The essays in this book were composed independently of each other, under no constraint other than that they were required to be original exercises in comparative popular culture. As will be seen, they differ in methodology, approaching their subjects from perspectives ranging from the historical to the aesthetic to the social scientific; they compile

evidence ranging from the anecdotal to the analytical to the statistical. Taken together, then, they demonstrate that there are various ways to "do" effective comparative popular culture scholarship.

These nine essays, however, can be seen to have more in common than the fact that they share the same general subject-area. For one thing, each of them exhibits a more than scholarly interest in and empathy for the situation of another nation or people; they are, in the highest sense, "humanistic." Moreover, some of the conclusions to which these essays come may confound reader's suspicions or only confirm them, but all affirm to some extent the considerable degree of autonomy exhibited by each national group under study. In other words, every essay in its own way demonstrates the tendency of human beings: to put culture to their own personal, social, and national uses; to resist the imposition of values, beliefs, and attitudes that are not compatible with those of their milieux; and to translate and otherwise transform foreign popular culture and its attendant ideology into entertainment that meets their own needs, that affords them the kind of gratification they seek. From them it can be inferred, then, that despite the alarmists, international acculturation is far from automatic, far from total.

For example, four of these essays, in one way or the other, try to come to grips with the effects of ideology and/or national policy on the production, distribution, and consumption of popular culture. Chantal Cinquin's essay, "President Mitterand Also Watches *Dallas*," confronts these issues most directly. From her perspective as a former member of the French diplomatic service with responsibilities for cultural affairs, she is able to trace the history of U.S. policy with regard to the exportation of popular culture, particularly to Europe, since the end of World War II, as well as the evolution of the official responses of the French government to those policies and practices. The questions of "national identity," national and international culture, and "cultural pluralism" that her essay raises bear directly or indirectly on all of the pieces that follow.

Wendy Pfeffer's essay on American and French game shows, "Intellectuals Are More Popular in France," offers a concrete example of the kind of Americanization of the global village that, as Professor Cinquin shows, has seriously concerned the government of France, among others. Professor Pfeffer notes that the favor such American programs as *The Wheel of Fortune* have won with French audiences has resulted in their surpassing the more academic game shows popular for so long in France and so reflective (according to the French) of their more intellectual national character. The prospect that the French Vanna White could become more of a national icon than Simone de Beauvoir raises the question as to the validity of older concepts of "national identity" in the age of the global village.

Closer to home, however content the Mexican government has been over the years to submit to American influence, Mexican intellectuals and artists have long objected to the Yankeefication of their country. Their particular concern has been with the wholesale importation of gringo ideology, particularly in the form of popular culture from *Los Estados Unidos*. In his essay, "Images of the United States in Selected Mexican Comic Books," Charles Tatum records objections from the left that even the comic book has become a vehicle of American propaganda and imperialism, yet shows that such objections may not be well-founded. His case in point: one of the most popular Mexican comic books is a wholly native product and in fact features an ongoing satiric critique of U.S. policies, practices, and citizens. Ironically, a medium invented in the U.S.A. becomes in Mexican hands a tool for subverting gringoism. This essay also serves as a reminder then that, however comforting the idea of the global village may be, its reality can be fraught with tensions.

A second group of essays turns the tables, showing not so much how American popular culture may exploit and manipulate other peoples as how other peoples have employed American popular culture and technology for their own purposes. Thus, in "Cat People and Mean Streets," Joan Worley demonstrates how a German moviemaker and an Argentine novelist have responded to American *film noir*, making it at once a subject of their art, a commentary upon the American experience, and a vehicle for contemplating the relationship between art and life. In the process, neither the mode nor its message remains unchanged.

Yolanda Broyles González's essay also deals with the appropriation of a foreign culture, but in a very different way. In "Cheyennes in the Black Forest: A Social Drama," she analyzes the German fascination with the American Indian, particularly the efforts by certain working-class Germans actually to re-enact the lifestyle of the American Plains Indian as a leisure-time pursuit. Drawing upon current theories in social anthropology as well as oral histories gathered among such "German Indians," Professor Broyles González shows how German blue-collar workers who do not identify with official "high German culture" symbolically express and perhaps ease their social alienation by recreating the life-customs of another oppressed people, made familiar to them through countless American films and popular German novels.

The American and West German receptions of *Holocaust* are compared in the essay by Bruce A. Murray. Through his analysis of this American docudrama, of West German film and television images of the Third Reich, and newspaper and magazine stories about *Holocaust,* Professor Murray shows that national history as well as national character affects how a people "process" an artifact of popular culture: whereas American responses to *Holocaust* revolved mainly around the national ethos, stressing the moral rightness of U.S. opposition to the Nazis and their values, in West Germany, still trying to deal with its global guilt, the informational and educational values of the series received the strongest emphasis. On the other hand, in his essay, "Singing against Hunger…"André Prévos finds that such basic matters as geography, the organization of the popular culture industry, and available technology go a long way toward determining how a popular artifact is created and "consumed" in Germany, France, England, the United States, or elsewhere. The subject Professor Prévos focuses upon is the series of rock concerts organized specifically to provide financial and other aid to the unfortunate. His approach is eclectic (as comparative popular culture study usually must be), ranging from the collection and analysis of hard data to the interpretation of the lyrics of songs written especially for these concerts.

Two essays that illustrate how popular culture can be seen as a special kind of expression of the "family of man," responding to fundamental human desires and needs that transcend geopolitical boundaries, conclude this volume. *Glasnost,* for example, will probably never completely ease the tensions between the U.S. and the U.S.S.R., but it is beginning to blur some of the distinctions between American and Russian TV. Or so one could conclude from Heidi Karriker's comparison of American and Russian television programming, "And Now, He-e-e-e-re's Misha! Soviet Television Since *Perestroika.*" Always in the background of such analyses is an issue, not so much of national character as of national policy: though both may appear to have entertainment and information as their main purposes, in fact Americans use the medium of television primarily to make a profit, whereas the Soviets employ this American invention primarily to make propaganda. Propaganda, direct and indirect, is of course not unknown to American television, and the budget allotted to state television by the Soviet Ministry of Culture presumably has its limitations, so both systems do have some systemic things in common. Both also recognize the importance of entertaining their audiences in effecting their ends. Nevertheless, as Professor Karriker's essay indicates, in the era of Gorbachev, Soviet TV is beginning to look more and more like its Western counterparts. "And Now, He-e-e-e-re's Misha!" serves as a good example of one of the chief values of comparative popular culture: not only does it provide us with information about other peoples and their societies not readily available elsewhere, but by so doing it illuminates our own society and ourselves.

Finally, Christine A. Holmund's essay reveals a surprising similarity between *La grande illusion,* a classic French film of the 1940's and the enormously successful American movie of the 1970s, *Rocky.* Of course, alongside the fact that a lot of American film and television is very popular abroad is another: that for years various kinds of English movies and television, Oriental science fiction and martial arts films, and many

European actors, musicians, dancers, and their works have become extremely popular in the United States. What this seems to say is that today, more so than ever before, there is 1) a universal appetite for popular culture, and 2) that appetite can often be satisfied by products that do not necessarily emerge out of one's national culture. Professor Holmlund's essay also explores the implications of such facts for teaching—yet another area where comparative popular culture can be used to "raise consciousness."

One of the ways in which it is common to distinguish elite culture from popular culture, the "masterpieces" from the "trash," is that there is supposed to be something universal, something that transcends time and space, about a "classic." "Great" art and letters, it is said, strike chords in all peoples in all ages—and that is why they become canonical. The evidence for this claim is weak in the extreme, yet as an article of faith it endures and even prevails. The evidence—quantifiable, verifiable, and therefore (so it would seem) not readily dismissable— that a lot of popular culture also has such widespread appeal and thus must also evince a kind of "resonance" throughout the family of man— tends to be ignored. Fortunately, essays like that of Professor Holmlund and the others in this book can help to correct the erroneous impression that culture exists in various mutually exclusive and variously valued categories, including national categories. For, if the essays in this book implicitly make one collective statement, it is that in a profound sense "culture is one."

No essays comparing African, say, or Oriental popular culture with its American counterparts are to be found in this volume. None, unfortunately, were submitted, and thus the true universality of much popular culture cannot be as convincingly demonstrated in these pages as it might have been. Moreover, this book cannot even hint at what might be learned about societies more different from our own than those of Latin America and Europe (upon which it mainly focuses), nor at what their use of popular culture can tell us about our own. But if it is only a beginning, this book is at least that, a beginning. There is much more work in comparative popular culture to do, and perhaps it will be done somewhat more efficiently and effectively thanks to the foundation the authors of the essays which follow have laid.

Postscript: For Comparative Literature and
Foreign Language Scholars in Particular

What the popular culture movement may need now is the equivalent of the famous World War I Uncle Sam poster for comparative popular culture studies. Whatever its art work, "Comparative Popular Culture Wants You!" would figure prominently in its text. In finer print it might extend a special invitation to foreign language and comparative literature scholars to begin to take up comparative popular culture. As noted earlier, it is they, after all, who are probably best suited for exploring the *terra incognita* that foreign popular culture largely is. Such a poster would not, of course, ignore those social scientists and humanists already doing popular culture scholarship but who thus far have confined their attention to their own nation's products.

The challenges posed by rigorous comparative popular culture scholarship are arguably greater than those usually posed by more traditional work, but the potential benefits are commensurately larger. For, while it is true that, by studying their national popular culture, Americans may gain insights into their complex national character and the melting pot of their national community, it is also true that by comparing and contrasting our national popular culture to others we come to know the rest of our world better. And that—in the Age of the Global Village—means to know ourselves better.

Part I:
In The Global Village,
The Natives are Restless

—*French ambivalence about American popular culture*

—*"Wheel of Fortune" versus the classic French game show, "Des chiffres et des lettres"*

—*Satire on all things gringo in the comic books of Mexican artist, "Rius"*

President Mitterrand Also Watches *Dallas*: American Mass Media and French National Policy

Chantal Cinquin

In Mexico, at the 1982 General Conference of UNESCO, French Culture Minister Jack Lang blamed a "system of financial and multinational domination" for "no longer appropriating only territories but peoples' trains of thought, ways of life." Lang went on to vehemently advocate the creation of an international association of "national cultures" which would oppose "the imperialism of financial groups." He condemned "some of these powerful nations that have no other moral standards but those of profit, and that attempt to impose a homogeneous culture on a planetary scale" (*Journal* 6-7).

The United States was not named by Lang but was clearly if indirectly being indicted for its policy concerning the technologies of communication. As *The Wall Street Journal* humorously pointed out: "What other country possessed the means and the marketing to pollute the fatherland of Molière with *Dallas?* Clearly, we vulgar Yanks, were Mr. Lang's cultural conquistadors" ("Changing" 24).

The long term steady American commercial exploitation of the French film market was what the Culture Minister particularly opposed, reproaching the U.S. for using cinema as a "mode of interference in the interior affairs of other countries, and more seriously, in the consciousness of the citizens of those countries" (1982, 5). Lang did not document his charges, but his comparing commercial communication to political interference did add to the existing European repertoire of anti-American themes.

Only two years after his Mexico speech, however, the same Lang inaugurated a French film festival in New York. On this occasion, while speaking with American journalists, he retracted his former statement. He even went so far as to withdraw the word "imperialism" he had used in Mexico, concerning which he regretted "an unfortunate misunderstanding due to the American oversensitivity to certain words when they come out of the mouth of French officials" ("Changing"

12

24). In New York, Lang praised the "dialogue" between the French and American cultures and called for the development of cultural exchanges between the two nations. Two years after the Mexican incident, this dramatic change of attitude suggested the abandonment of simplistic anti-Americanism and the charting of new directions for French cultural policy.

This essay will examine the successor to Lang's 1982 anti-Americanism, the concept of "cultural identity", a cause and a political program that Jack Lang would champion until the end of his mandate in March 1986. But first and more generally, the central role of mass media in Franco-American relations will be considered.

1. The Conquest of Minds

Jack Lang's Mexican invectives, widely echoed by the international press, were not without precedents. French anti-Americanism with regard to movies has a long history. The grievances voiced in 1982 against American leadership in audio-visual communication reiterated themes expressed as early as 1946. It will be worthwhile to go back to the postwar state of Franco-American cultural relations to explain both their continuity and their rupture in 1982.

The plan of economic aid designed by the Americans for the reconstruction of wartorn France contained a clause relative to the film industry: the French were to open up their national film market to American productions without any reciprocal exchange. An importation quota stipulated that movie theaters in France should not screen more than four French films every three months for at least two years. The American film industry benefitted from these official arrangements on two accounts: 1) it had less to fear from French competition; 2) by eliminating the old quotas, the field was left open to American films, not only on the French market but in Europe as well, because measures of restriction of cinematographic creation had also been applied to Great Britain, Italy and Germany. (France did obtain the best deal, since it retained 30% of its national production whereas Great Britain had only 22% and Italy 17%.)

At this time, everything was favorable to the expansion of the American cinema. From 1939 to 1944, Hollywood had released more than 2000 films, while during the same wartime period in Europe production had been almost non-existent. American movies could also be offered at extremely competitive prices because their production expenses had already been recouped on the vast U.S. market. It would be misleading to see mere coincidence here, one that happened to be economically unfavorable to Europe. It is reasonable to infer that the American negotiators included the clause on film quotas in the treaty of economic assistance to Europe in part with the idea of using Hollywood as a means of political influence. Thus, in 1946, for the first time in Western history, a concern with *cultural* factors was directly linked to a global political and ideological plan (as would also be the case in 1982, with Jack Lang's statements). Popular culture was considered to be a crucial political weapon; thus, the respective positions of the United States in 1946 and of France in 1982 regarding the cultural battle are not very much at variance.

The extent of American dominance in the movies from 1946 to 1982 can be documented, as can the dramatic change following Lang's 1982 address. In 1946 the American administration was concerned with finding alternatives to military intervention in order to meet the threat of communism, one that, according to a report to President Truman, seemed ready to spread all over Europe:

The United States should support and assist all democratic countries which are in any way menaced or endangered by the USSR. Providing military support in case of attack is a last resort; a more effective barrier to communism is strong economic support...Our policy on reparations should be directed toward strengthening the areas we are endeavoring to keep outside the Soviet sphere. ("American" 67)

Popular Culture would come to be regarded as a subtle but effective additional weapon in such an overall strategy of containment. The procedure agreed upon consisted of utilizing "indirect propaganda," employing movies to circulate persuasive positive images of the American way of life abroad. In a 1946 article in *The New York Times,* Thomas Pryor, Director of Paramount Pictures, acknowledged Hollywood's new strategic foreign mission in rhetoric combining democratic ideals and foreign policy considerations:

We, the industry, recognize the need for informing people in foreign lands about the things that have made America a great country and we think we know how to put across the message of our democracy. ("Mission" 6)

The objective, defined and made clearer during the Cold War was:

to produce in the minds of potential adversaries, as well as potential allies of the American people, attitudes which would facilitate the evolution of a congenial international environment for the United States. (Gaddis 30)

These declarations and the measures that followed outraged the French press. Accusations of manipulation, interference and propaganda grew in number as the United States was seen to be taking advantage of France's ailing economy to impose its policy. In view of the decline of the French film industry from 1946 on, movie actors Jean Marais, Madeleine Sologne, Simone Signoret, Louis Jouvet and others demonstrated in the streets of Paris with anti-American slogans. The

respect local traditions had been strongly felt. The developing countries especially had come to accept the notion that their national growth should be perceived not only in economic, but also in cultural terms. The Mexico Conference put forward the political parameters relevant to international cultural exchanges, parameters which were very much in the foreground of the international scene because of the media coverage of Lang's speech. A worldwide awareness emerged with regard to the important role of cultural factors in all regions, including those where, until recently, they had been considered to be unimportant—in the development of Third-World countries. Four months after the Mexico Conference, the Director General of UNESCO, Amadou M. M'Bow declared:

The most recent reflections on development show that it becomes totally comprehensible only when the cultural dimension of a nation has been given consideration. For it is from culture that development receives its founding impetus; it is culture which provides peoples with motivations and energy; it is culture at last which can help define the style of development (6).

The protection of cultural identity in the 1980s is a primary political issue for most nations. The assertion of cultural identity, in the past, was seen as expressing the desire of formerly colonized countries to retain their popular traditions in the face of the culture imposed on them by their colonizers. Nowadays cultural identity as a concept has been redirected, given the current context: it epitomes a concern, at the governmental level, for the traumatizing effects of cultural hegemony as well as a determination to preserve a national consciousness. Terms borrowed from an earlier anticolonialist repertoire have been reworked and adapted to the current state of international relations. "Financial and cultural imperialism," "The colonization of radio and TV channels," "the right to resist the colonization of information," were phrases used by Lang in 1982 to indict United States without naming it (_Conference_ 6).

Which were the colonized and which the colonizing countries was not specified by the French Culture Minister. But Europe as well as the developing countries were represented by Lang as being subjected to a supposed cultural dictatorship made in the United States. Lang's militant vocabulary also applied to a situation in which cultural exchanges were becoming dominated by the computer market, by electronics and by the satellite networks. Figures in these sectors speak for themselves: American firms provide 84% of French computers: they control about 70% of the world data banks and 50% of the world market in electronics; the European computer industry depends on foreign permits for 97% of its production and the European Economic Community manufactures only half of the electronic parts it needs. These facts then make the question raised by Régis Debray quite legitimate: "Can the computerization of the French society be something else but the denationalization of this society" (152)?

The problems posed by the development of communication technologies are not strictly of a technical or economic order. They are importantly political. In 1971, in his book *The Technotronic Revolution*, Z. Bzrezinski foresaw a de facto and de jure internationalization of all the world's nations. This would be accomplished by the advances of computer science and electronics. Brzezinski called for the suppression of national borders, perceived as archaïc remnants of a by-gone world: "Words such as capitalism, democracy, socialism and communism—and even nationalism—do no longer make much sense" (152).

Such a statement helps to explain basic grievances formulated against UNESCO, notably by Jean B. Gerard, the last American ambassador to UNESCO (1984). In an article giving the reasons for the American withdrawal from UNESCO, she contrasts "human rights," supported by the United States, to "peoples' rights," which she rejects as an arbitrary notion used by other governments to take an ideological adversarial stand against the free world:

Instead of being bound to protect their citizens against the misuse of state power, under the aegis of the human rights such as we know them, the governments are granted rights which take over the rights of the individuals. The individuals who represent private interests without claiming to embody those of the overall people—journalists, union leaders, industry executives, plain citizens or poets—could be refused the right to speak freely, if their views opposed the peoples' rights to solidarity or cultural identity...Although we all respect the right to self-determination and national sovereignty, I am prone to think that the obscure "peoples' right" does not mean more nowadays than arbitrary absolutism without appeal. (28)

This analysis is in keeping with that of Z. Brzezinski. By dissociating human rights from the peoples' right, Gerard illuminates the limits and ambiguities of the notion of "cultural identity." The social problematics of identity tend to function according to a dialectic of "same" and "other," of belonging v.s. excluding. The many pitfalls of the cultural identity primary are, at home, the denial of liberties to artists and intellectuals and the negation of minority cultures; and abroad, nationalism, as well as constraints upon cultural communication. This danger is most manifest in nations where the claim to cultural identity is linked to a totalitarian global political scheme.

However, preference given to human rights over the peoples' right also ideally serves American objectives of external policy defined during the Cold War, according to which the American leadership in communication technologies is turned into a device of ideological exportation serving American interests.

Concrete measures have accompanied the American advocacy of the principle of the free spread of ideas as a universal principle, one that has precedence even over the principle of national sovereignty. Since 1945, the United States has used the platform of international organizations like UNESCO and the UNO, to prevent the international regulation of communication. Since the 1970's however, this ideology of the free circulation of information has lost its appeal to other nations. Against it, Third World countries and Europe as well took a united stand, strongly supporting alternative notions such as "balanced circulation," "national sovereignty," "reciprocity," and "opposition to unequal cultural exchange." Jack Lang's speech in Mexico then drew upon enduring post-war themes.

The American counterattack to this generalized offensive was to urge other nations to concentrate all their effort on technological matters and to oppose what the U.S. termed the "politicization of cultural exchanges." The goal thus aimed at, of course, was to turn social problems into purely technical questions and therefore to reinforce the dominant role of the American experts.

Countering the official American stand, the French government at the Sorbonne, in February 1983, brought together "women and men of culture" from all over the world—writers, artists, historians, economists, industrialists and sociologists—to discuss the theme (also the title) of the colloquium, *Creation and Development*. In the presence of President Mitterrand and Culture Minister Lang, the two-day conference was designed to lay down the principles of an international cultural policy whose objectives Lang said should be: "to prevent market mechanisms and the economic power struggle from imposing stereotyped, culturally meaningless products on individuals of other nations" (1983, 26). Jacques Attali, an advisor to Lang, formulated the following question for the participants' reflection: "May not development destroy creativity: does not economy risk squandering culture, robbing it or its originality by turning it into a commodity like any other, into a source of profit?" (28).

The same statement and question, a few years earlier, would have been directed (or interpreted) against the U.S. But in 1983, a consensus has been established, not so much on the basis of a negative anti-capitalistic or anti-American criticism, as out of a determination to define a political and cultural counterpower to the commercial interests of pressure groups.

The declarations of the participants of the Sorbonne colloquium gave a clear account of the evolution of the concept of cultural identity. In the 1970's, it was used as a substitute for the anti-Americanism of the 1950s-1960s. The aims of a strong anti-American ideology backed by the wide audience of the left-wing parties in Europe and the developing countries have been adapted to the up-to-date state of the international context. It was still this militant interpretation of the cultural identity that was taken up again by Lang in Mexico, but it is noteworthy that public opinion did not follow the French Culture Minister. Then, at the Sorbonne, in 1983, cultural identity merged with another concept, that of "cultural democracy." If cultural identity has strong nationalistic overtones, cultural democracy belongs to a different societal problematics.

In the perspective of cultural democracy, the full realization of the individual is regarded as essential for collective development. In this respect, Daniel Bell's prophecy came true. In *The Cultural Contradictions of Capitalism* (1973), Bell revealed how industrial growth and the organizing strategies of the technocratic state dramatically affect the communicational structures which govern the life of the community. He saw that in the near future the reaction to forced modernization would be a return to popular traditions that offer positive identification and existential certainty to the masses.

The participants of the Sorbonne colloquium confirmed this view. They condemned the process of the degeneration of the life experience imposed by economic imperatives, the progressive destabilization of urban and natural environments, the depreciation of great popular traditions. Cultural democracy was then assigned the mission of delivering on the promise of happiness that economic progress is unable to hold. Lang, indeed, asserts that culture is the solution to the economic crisis. He understands cultural identity as conviviality, stressing its existential dimension.

The hedonistic utopia of the reconciliation of man and the world often mentioned by Lang involves a political re-tooling of leftist ideology, focusing now on the individual rather than on the group. The continuation of this vision falls within a liberal concept of social relations. There is a logical progression in this scheme. The ultraculturalism of the left political figures who came into power in France in 1981 was expressed by such declarations as this one by Mitterand: "Socialism is first a cultural program," or this one by Lang: "The government is composed of forty Culture Ministers." This general attitude was bound to generate a new style of official pragmatism, namely cultural democracy. Once the nationalistic content of cultural identity had faded away and a consensus emerged for the benefit of the individual, anti-Americanism was no longer needed, ideologically speaking.

Cultural identity then was regarded not only as a means of resisting the alienation caused by the influence of those countries dominating the international scene, but also as the solution to internal social crisis. The rebalancing of the economic and cultural sectors within societies in general seemed particularly needed, according to anthropologist Jean Ki-Zerbo, speaking on behalf of the African nations: "Someone who would succeed in linking up economic growth with the inexhaustible cultural energy of the Africans would have invented the ideal engine of the continent's take-off" (164).

The same issue of the coordination of market strategies and cultural innovation is one that François Mitterand proposed to address: "Investing in culture means investing in economy. It frees the future and thus contributes to giving back to life its whole meaning" (1983,368). The position adopted during the Sorbonne conference comes within the frame of the overall cultural policy implemented by the French socialist government.

As soon as he was named Culture Minister, Jack Lang resolutely strove to eradicate prejudices that in France have long militated in favor of a separation—even an antagonism—between economy and culture. Industry executives approached economic development from an exclusively quantitative perspective which frequently underrated the role of artistic creation as a source of national growth and influence. As for the cultural sector itself, the legitimate concern for asserting cultural rights over short-term profitability often led to a wholesale rejections of commercial distribution, fund-raising, self-financing, or of business's participation in cultural life. Jack Lang's policies, from 1981 to 1985, brought about a drastic change in those attitudes and behaviors. The cornerstone of the Socialist' cultural policy has been the definition, development and backing of cultural industries. In this matter, the French, abandoning any ideological bias, were prompted to turn to the United States as to a model of society that might give them the clues they needed. A dramatic change of attitude was symbolized by Lang's use of an American economist as an authority to defend his cultural program and to obtain a significant increase of the Culture Ministry budget. Facing a skeptical Parliament, Lang said: "Twenty years ago, a very reputable American economist, Fritz Machulp, wondered which was the principal American industry. Was it steel, oil, chemistry, automobile? No, it was the industry of knowledge" (1982a). From a negative example, the United States had become a very useful example to follow.

The paradoxical character of Franco-American cultural relations from the late 1940's to the 80's is worth noticing. The national cultural consensus in France has been reached either by rejecting the American design of society or by adopting it.

The shift in the French political line discussed in this essay happened at a time when the influence of the Communist Party had much receded and when the Socialists had to acknowledge the validity of rightist positions on economy. It reflects the compromise of "cohabitation" and the general indictment of state-controlled life. At this writing (1988), in France the only issue is the renewed sense that the French left and right alike want to give to democracy. We have examined the content of cultural democracy put forward by Lang. The minister of Economy and Finances, Edouard Balladur, has also defined a fiscal democracy, an economic democracy, a stock market democracy, and added new meaning to the concept of "cultural democracy" when he presented his bill on art patronage at the National Assembly, in the spring of 1987. Balladur also issued a book entitled *I Believe In Man More Than In The State* (1987). The title is rather unexpected and challenging from a previous E.N.A. (Ecole Nationale d' Administration) scholar and top civil servant under Presidents Pompidou and Mitterrand. It is, however, quite representative of the awareness in today's French society of the primacy of the individual. This is a new phase in the everlasting conflict in French politics between civil society and state power.

From this perspective, the massive success of *Dallas* reveals an unquestionable popular aspiration. The TV series is built along the line of an advertising message. The plot is to a large extent a vehicle designed to display the consumption practices of an upper-class American family. The spectacle of unrestricted consumption represents a successfull strategy of social integration. So when Mitterrand declares that he also watches *Dallas* and enjoys it, does he not mean that he is willing to take into account the individuals' desire to unlimited welfare, even at the price of capitalism? He admits that, contrary to a centralizing tradition, the socialist state too should limit the authoritarian dynamics proper to the economic and administrative systems to the benefit of the individuals.

Not without a hint of paradox and, at any rate, not without ideological inconsistency, it has been a socialist regime which, after first inveighing against American cultural domination and interference in other nations, has come to advocate the adoption of liberal options inspired by the United States.

Works Cited

Attali, Jacques. *Création et Développement,* Paris: Archives of the Culture Ministry. Unpublished proceedings of the conference, 1983.

Balladur, Edouard. *Je crois plus en l'homme qu'en l'Etat,* Paris: Flammarion, 1987.

Bell, Daniel. *The Coming of the Postindustrial Society,* New York: Basic Books Inc., 1976.

Brzezinski, Zbigniew. *La révolution technotronique* Paris: Calman Lévy, (1971) cited in *Debray* op. cit, 1984.

Debray, Régis. *La puissance et les rêves* Paris: Gallimard, 1984.

De la Salle, Bertrand. "As a Frenchman sees us" in *La Nation* March 15, 1947.

Eudes, Yves. *La conquête des esprits* Paris: Maspero, 1982.

Gaddis, John. *Containment: Documents on American Policy and Strategy, 1945-50* New York: Columbia University Press, 1978.

Gerard, Jean B. "Pourquoi les Etats-Unis ont dû quitter l'UNESCO" _Revue des Deux Mondes_, Paris: June 1984, cited in _L'UNESCO en question_, Paris: Documentation Française, 1985.

Guilbaut, Serge. _How New York Stole the Idea of Modern Art_, Chicago: The University of Chicago Press, 1983.

Ki-Zerbo, Jean. _Création et Développement_, Paris: Archives of the Culture Ministry. Unpublished proceedings of the conference, 1983.

Lang, Jacques. "Changing Tunes at the French Culture Ministry" in the Wall Street Journal, January 17, 1985.

_____ _Création et développement_ Paris: Archives of the Culture Ministry. Unpublished, 1983.

_____ _Journal Officiel du 3 novembre 1982_ Paris: Archives of the French Culture Ministry. Unpublished, 1982.

_____ _Conférence de Mexico. Juillet 1982_ Paris: Archives of the Culture Ministry. Unpublished, 1982.

Loomis, Harry S. _USIA Operations_, Washington DC: US Government Printing Office, cited in Yves Eudes (1982) op. cit., 1971.

M'Bow, Amadou M. "Introduction au débat général sur le Plan 1984-1989 à la quatrième session of la Conférence Générale", November 24, 1982 cited in _L'UNESCO en question_ Paris: La Documentation Française, 1985.

Mitterand, Françoise _Création et Développement_, Paris: Archives of the Culture Ministry. Unpublished, 1983.

_____ "Rapport au sommet des pays industrialisés: Technique, croissance, emploi" Versailles, June 1982, cited in _Le projet culturel extérieur de la France_, Ministère des Relations Estérieures ed. Paris: LaDocumentation Française, 1982.

Pryor, Thomas M. "Mission of the Movies Abroad", New York Times, March 29 1946, cited in _Guilbaut_ (1983) op. cit., 1983.

Truman, Harry S. "American Relations with the Soviet Union. A Report to the President" June 1946, cited in _Gaddis_ op. cit., 1978.

Intellectuals Are More Popular in France: The Case of French and American Game Shows

Wendy Pfeffer

French culture, even French popular culture, is profoundly intellectual, in its poses if not in reality. The French have long taken pride in their cultural heritage, and refuse to admit that Paris is no longer the center of the intellectual world, just as many French have difficulty admitting that Paris has not been the center of the art world since the end of World War II. This cultural and intellectual heritage is impressed on French children in school. For many French high school students, for example, philosophy is a required course, tested on the high school exit exam, the *baccalauréat*. Even high school math majors are required to take a large dose of literature, and the essay questions asked on the *baccalauréat* would cause many American college graduates to pale. The French system attempts to mold students into an educated and enlightened intelligentsia, capable of participating in the intellectual and cultural life of their country.

In keeping with this emphasis, books and magazines have a visibility and importance in France that is unmatched in the United States. As Mimi Kramer has written, "[In France] everyone believes in the magic status of the *homme de lettres*" (87). She quotes one book critic who says that "le chemin de la gloire passe par la littérature" (87; the road to glory goes via literature). This emphasis on the print media can be seen in the variety of French daily newspapers and weekly news magazines, variety unmatched in the United States either in number or political slant ("Read Less About It" 37). Although 70% of the French avoid newspapers entirely and learn about the news from television, the print media remain important ("Read Less About It" 37).

So too, the annual Salon du Livre, the French book show, is not so much a trade show for professionals, as is the Frankfurt Book Fair, but an opportunity for individuals to see and purchase new books. School children are brought to the Salon by their teachers and presented books by publishers eager to encourage reading. The Salon du Livre has been

24

so successful in its seven years of existence that the Grand Palais, some 5,000 square meters of exposition space in Paris, is now too small for the Salon, which must find a new home for the 1988 show.

Another example: *Télérama* is essentially a television magazine, providing information on the coming week's broadcasts. But it also includes book reviews, record and movie reviews; its special edition for the Paris region includes articles on historic landmarks or local cultural events.

This intellectual and cultural tradition has long been reflected in French television programming. Writing on the development in France of television talk shows, Lise Bloch-Morhange observes, "Chaque pays ayant la télévision qu'il mérite, ce n'est pas un hasard si, chez nous, les plus belles réussites...sont, jusqu'à présent, chacune dans un registre plutôt 'intello' " (16; Since each country has the television it deserves, it's not by chance that in France, the most successful [talk shows] are, up to now, rather "intellectual" in tone). The closest American equivalent to French television programming of the 1960's and 1970's is found on Public Broadcasting Service (PBS) stations, known as "educational television" to distinguish it from the other American networks.

Perhaps the best example of the intellectual nature of French broadcasting is *Apostrophes,* broadcast on Friday evenings in prime time on Antenne 2, where four or five authors discuss their latest works with the host, Bernard Pivot, who has become a celebrity as a result of this program. The show is pointedly intellectual, a factor noted by Lech Walesa, the Polish shipyard electrical worker and leader of Solidarity, the once banned Polish workers' union, when he was interviewed by Pivot for the show (broadcast April 24, 1987; see also Bloch-Morhange 16). When asked why he was wearing a necktie, since such is not his normal practice, Walesa said that all French intellectuals watch *Apostrophes,* and for them, he wore the tie. The French were proud to have arranged publication of Walesa's autobiography, and it is clear that Walesa was familiar enough with *Apostrophes* to know the audience he would be addressing that evening.

Books featured on *Apostrophes* are described in the various television magazines, occasionally with a feature article, regularly with a plot summary or brief description and a short biography of the author. These books are also featured in French bookstores, with special "Featured on *Apostrophes*" displays. No one will deny that there is competition to appear on this show, since, as this interviewer was told in a major Paris bookstore, book sales increase following an *Apostrophes* appearance (see also Kramer 87).

In a related vein, and in keeping with this intellectual emphasis, Bernard Pivot has launched a campaign to improve French orthography. His campaign, nationally broadcast, consists of a competitive dictation exam. After several initial quizzes, contestants are gathered in all parts of France to listen to Pivot read, on television, the semi-final. A month later, the finalists meet in Paris for a reading of the final dictation, a text larded with spelling tricks and grammar potholes, again broadcast on national television. The prizes, not surprisingly, are books. This dictation exam, a classic school exercise, is treated by the sponsoring national television channel as a major Saturday event, complete with coverage at remote sites and with the participation of "celebrity" competitors.

Game shows created in France for television reflect the Gallic scholastic tradition. These programs emphasize intellectual ability and discount the show-business aspect of television in their design. They tend to have amateurish sets and lack electrical buzzers, flashing lights, or fancy props. The classic French game show, *Des chiffres et des lettres*, depends on its Master of Ceremonies to reveal nine letters chosen at random by the two contestants—cardboard letters which are then posted on a felt board. These letters must then be arranged into words, but each letter can be used only once in the word. The word using the most posted letters wins the most points. (All words proposed are verified by two judges who use recent one-volume dictionaries; Le Parc, "Le jeu" 4.)

Alternating with the word game is a mathematical skill game. Six numbers are chosen, again at random, again posted on a felt board. Then the hostess pushes three buttons to generate a three-digit number. The contestants must combine the six numbers they have chosen, by addition, subtraction, multiplication or division, in order to arrive at the three-digit figure. Points are awarded based on how many of the six numbers are used in the calculation (each number can be used only once). The winner is the first contestant to accumulate 100 points. Prize money on this show is negligible, and the pace of the show, by American standards, lethargic. (In a recent effort to increase the pace of the show, the time contestants had to compose their answers was reduced from forty-five to forty seconds [Bailly 21].) And yet *Des chiffres et des lettres* has been on the air in its current format for over fifteen years.

One notable difference between this show and its American counterparts is that the studio audience of *Des chiffres et des lettres* is frequently invited to do the contestants one better when the "official" players in the game have come up with an answer short of perfect (a word of six letters when one of eight can be created, for example). An announcer stands ready in the aisles to report to the Master of Ceremonies the answers proposed by observers in the studio, all of whom are avid fans of the game.

The United States, on the other hand, has traditionally valued the acquisition of wealth more than the demonstration of intellectual knowledge, and this tradition is reflected in U.S. television programming. Even those American shows that test intellectual ability put more emphasis on the money or prizes to be won than on the skills of the contestants. In fact, the common denominator of all American game shows is cash or prizes. Consider *Jeopardy*, whose premise is that contestants must furnish questions to the answers provided on the gameboard. The answers are "hidden" under different dollar amounts, so that this show, which does require contestants to demonstrate some general knowledge, nonetheless has contestants select answers on the gameboard chosen by dollar value.

Another program, *WordPlay*, supposedly tests contestants' knowledge of English vocabulary. Contestants pick a word from the game board, and the three guest stars each provide definitions for the word, only one of which is accurate. Rarely are the contestants familiar with the words in the game (which range from the simple to the truly esoteric); most often, contestants are guessing which definition is correct. Nonetheless, contestants are really interested in the dollar value hidden under a given word and are encouraged to pick the word under which is hidden the bonus cash prize.

The preoccupation with gaining wealth is such that the expertise demanded on one program, *The Price is Right,* is an accurate and wide-ranging familiarity with the retail cost of the prizes to be won. On *Bargain Hunters,* contestants are expected to know whether the price posted on a prize is the actual selling price, or whether they are getting "a bargain" by purchasing the item at the posted price. The winner on this show is the contestant who manages to "save" the most money on his "purchases."

Characteristically, American shows do not test "book knowledge," learning acquired in school, but rather trivia picked up in the streets, or, more often, in shopping centers. American contestants are chosen for their ability to be animated on camera, rather than for their knowledge. The typical American set is professional, often flashy. Neither the studio nor the home audience is actively involved in the game; the American television audience is expected to be passive. *Bargain Hunters* is exceptional in that it encourages home viewers to participate in the program: viewers can dial a toll-free number to purchase merchandise advertised on the show. Audience participation takes the form of acquisition, not intellectual challenge. But then, the audience does not expect a mental challenge; the spectacle is the entertainment.

France is currently remodeling what has been dubbed the *PAF* *(paysage audio-visuel français,* "the shape of its audio-visual landscape"), and radical changes are occurring in television programming as a result.

Notably, the French government has sold to private investors one of the three "government channels," meaning that there are now two government channels and four private ones. This privatization of television has changed the nature of French television, most importantly because what was once a channel recognized as the voice of the government (Channel TF1) now represents private investors. Privatization has resulted in an increased number of channels directed at a general audience. Despite the government's efforts to control programming by defining the duties of each channel through the *cahier des charges*, "notebook of responsibilities," drafted by the Commission Nationale de la Communication et des Libertés, each channel has been forced to deal with the costs of production, the necessity of selling commercial space, and the problem of ratings. The result of all this is a longer programming day and an increased need for programs.

One solution for broadcasters is the importation of American programs, which may or may not be converted for French tastes. In some cases, importation has simply been a matter of dubbing French dialogue over English, as was done for *Dallas, Miami Vice, Santa Barbara, Who's the Boss?* and *Kate and Allie.*

Another approach to filling air time is to produce American shows in France. This is what happened to *The Wheel of Fortune,* imported as *La Roue de la fortune.* According to the producer of the French show, Marc Gurnaud, the American model has been copied to the letter. Gurnaud told this interviewer that he was never more proud than when the American crew visited his set and thought they were in Hollywood. The French master of ceremonies copied the behavior of the American m.c., Pat Sajak (putting his arm around contestants, for example) until viewer mail, protesting such familiarity, put an end to it. There was a national talent search for the hostess of the show, someone "one hundred percent French" in the words of Associate Producer Nadine Pouffary-Hermann, even though this same producer said what they were looking for was "a French Vanna White." Both the first host of the program, Michel Robbe, and Producer Marc Gurnaud have emphasized that the star of the show is not the host, but the game itself (Heitz, "La part du rêve" 129).

Most remarkable of all is *La Roue de la fortune's* emphasis on acquiring prizes, which stands in great contrast to traditional French gameshows. As Gurnaud explained to me, at first there was resistance to people winning things on television.[1] But gradually audiences have adapted, and Gurnaud has a backlog of some 500,000 letters from people who want to participate as contestants on the show.

Gurnaud stated that *La Roue de la fortune* was the start of a new era, not only for French game shows, but for French television in general. The important factor, henceforth, would be "American style." For

Gurnaud, American style means a production with minimal improvisation; everything happens quickly; there are no pauses, no moments of conversation between the host and hostess.

Gurnaud was emphatic in asserting that speed and dynamism are the marks of an American-style show. This emphasis on the show's momentum is such that contestants for *La Roue de la fortune* undergo a two-step selection process: a written test to determine their intellectual knowledge, and a second test, to see how well they have mastered the "dynamique du jeu," the "dynamism of the game." Similar tests are used in the U.S. for *The Wheel of Fortune.* Interestingly enough, it would appear that contestants are chosen much more for their mastery of the "dynamique du jeu" than for their intellectual ability. For example, the contestants on *La Roue de la Fortune* were unable to guess the name of France's premier tennis player, Yannick Noah, a national hero, until all but one letter of his name was revealed.

Gurnaud explained to me that for the show's questions, he tried to choose *énigmes,* "puzzles," from current events. During the period of the Cannes Film Festival, there was a preponderance of words and titles relating to the movies; during the Roland Garros Tennis Tournament, a preponderance of names from the world of tennis.

It should be stressed that, as of June 1, 1987, *La Roue de la fortune* was the only show with this kind of speed and dynamism broadcast in France. I asked Gurnaud if he thought French television was becoming more American; he answered in the negative. However, six months later, with even more American-style game shows being broadcast in France, it would appear that Gurnaud was wrong.

La Roue de la fortune has knocked its competition, *Des Chiffres et des lettres,* on its ear. During the first six months of 1987, the two shows were broadcast directly opposite each other. Within four weeks of its first broadcast, *La Roue de la Fortune* had surpassed *Des Chiffres et des lettres* in the ratings, and in May, *La Roue* had a regular audience of some 10 million viewers, compared to 8 million for *Des chiffres et des lettres.* Changed to a prime time slot just before the evening news, *La Roue de la fortune* continues to attract 10 to 12 million viewers each night. By way of comparison, *Apostrophes* has a regular viewing audience of 4 million.

The success of *La Roue de la fortune* has encouraged French television producers to import other American game shows. Some French producers had thought that French reserve would keep American-style game shows from succeeding, but they were soon proved wrong (Chemin 17). *The Price is Right* began broadcasting as *Le juste prix* on December 13, 1987. Its first studio audience cried, screamed, cheered, and applauded, in the manner of the best American audiences. Initially, *The Price is Right* was scheduled for broadcast on French cable television and was not expected to have the same impact as *La Roue de la fortune*. But *Le juste prix* is being broadcast on France's TF1, formerly the state channel, to a nation-wide audience that has greeted the show with gusto, notwithstanding negative public opinion about the amounts of money involved on these new television game shows.

Producer Gurnaud saw no problem in turning television away from its more intellectual pursuits. His parting line to me was, "Intellectuel c'est bien; distraire c'est mieux," "It's good to be intellectual; it's better to entertain." But others are concerned with the changes occurring on French television and in France in general. Pivot was able to organize an evening on *Apostrophes* where five authors did nothing more than criticize contemporary (popular) culture (broadcast 3 April 1987). To poke fun at developments in television programming and to celebrate the six-hundredth broadcast of *Apostrophes*, Pivot conducted his broadcast as normal, but followed the show with a fifteen-minute gameshow special, *Apostrophages*, a literary gameshow where famous authors sold their latest book in order to win washing machines or refrigerators (broadcast 20 November 1987, see D[uma]y 28).

Despite the evidence of ratings (*Apostrophes* a distant third to *Des chiffres et des lettres*, following *La Roue de la fortune*), "intellectual" programming is not dying in France. The 1986 national finals of *Des chiffres et des lettres* attracted an audience of some 16 million viewers (Audimat-Médiamétrie), still not the magnitude of the most-watched show that week, a French film comedy (40 million viewers), but the fourth most-watched show of the week.

It is unlikely that there is a cultural crisis in France, and that "intellectual" values have been abandoned. Certainly there remain what Franck Nouchi dubbed "cultural particularities" that distinguish France from the United States (16). As Nouchi noted, it is indicative that the first American celebrity to announce publicly his infection with AIDS was the actor Rock Hudson. In France, Nouchi continued, the parallel public announcement came from Jean-Paul Aron, noted author and sociologist.

While there may be changes occurring in France, and while popular culture in France may be becoming more similar to American popular culture, still there remains something about it that is distinctively French, uniquely intellectual. Some evidence for the vitality of the French intellectual tendency may be indicated by an event that occurred on April 1, 1987. During the evening news, one of the government's national television stations, Antenne 2, announced that Bernard Pivot had been named an officer of the government, responsible for the language of the French. Pivot declined to accept the title "Monsieur Langue," "Mr. Language,"[2] though he did accept the office, his main charge being to eliminate the use of English in French. In an interview broadcast during the same evening news show, Pivot announced that he was banning the use of initials or acronyms: words existed to be used to the full. *Télérama* ran a cover article on the appointment (Belot and Lecarpentier 6-12). Then for a month afterwards, Pivot, Antenne 2 and *Télérama* did their best to publicize disclaimers for what was no more than an elaborate April Fool's joke.

A joke perhaps, but in the best French intellectual tradition. It may be that the French will spend more and more time watching American-style gameshows, but they will bemoan this state of affairs with extended printed commentaries, to be discussed in the classroom and in the finest Paris salons.[3]

Notes

[1]The percentage of French who disapprove of the money involved on game shows has been increasing, according to public opinion polls conducted for *Télérama* and for *Communication et Business*. The figure was 70% in December 1987 (Chemin 17); one month later, in January 1988, it had risen to 75% (Labé 25).

[2]Jack Lang was Minister of Culture while the Socialists controlled the French Assemblée (1981-1986); Pivot was punning on his new title which rhymed with the name of the former minister.

[3]See in this regard, Remond 8-11 and Maury et al. 20-25.

Works Cited

"A nos lecteurs." *L'Evénement de jeudi* 7 April 1987: 121.

Audimat-Médiamétrie. "Les dix émissions les plus regardées." *Le Monde Radio-Télévision* [Paris, France] 15-16 February 1987.

Bailly, Laurent. "Les virtuoses du dictionnaire et de la table de multiplication." *Le Monde Radio-Télévision* [Paris, France] 28-29 September 1986: 21-22.

Belot, Jean and Marc Lecarpentier. "Enfin un contrôleur de la langue!" *Télérama* 1 April 1987: cover; 6-12.

Bloch-Morhange, Lise. "La parole comme spectacle." *Le Monde Radio-Télévision* [Paris, France] 24-25 January 1988: 16-17.

Chemin, Ariane. "La France joue et gagne." *Le Monde Radio-Télévision* 13-14 December 1987: 16-17.

"Des chiffres et des lettres." *Télérama* 28 January 1987: 96.

D[uma]y, J.-M. "Six cents bougies pour 'Apostrophes'." *Le Monde* [Paris, France] 20 November 1987: 28.

Garcin, Jérôme et al. "Culture: quand la télé parle à la télé."*L'Evénement de jeudi* 28 May 1987: 9-11.

Gurnaud, Marc. Personal interview. 26 May 1987.

Heitz, Bernard. "La part du rêve." *Télérama* 15 April 1987: 129.

———. "Robbe du soir." *Télérama* 21 January 1987.

Kramer, Mimi. "Letter from Europe." *New Yorker* 22 February 1988: 87-98

Labé, Yves-Marie. "Les téléspectateurs deviennent publiphobes." *Le Monde* [Paris, France] 11 February 1988: 25.

Le Parc, Denis. "Comment sont-ils sélectionnés." *Jeux de notre temps* May 1987: 4.

———. "Le jeu 'Des chiffres et ses lettres' et des règles."*Jeux de notre temps* June 1987: 4.

Maury, Serge et al. "Télé: le désastre." *L'Evènement de jeudi* 8-14 October 1987: cover, 20-25.

Nouchi, Franck. "SIDA et médias." *Le Monde* [Paris, France] 1-2 November 1987: 16.

Pouffary-Hermann, Nadine. Personal interview. 26 May, 1987.

"Read Less About It." *The Economist* 30 January 1988: 36-37.

Remond, Alain. "La culture déboussolée? Quatre penseurs courent après." *Télérama* 6 June 1987: cover, 8-11.

Images of the United States in Selected Mexican Comic Books

Charles Tatum

Ariel Dorfman and Armand Mattelart's 1972 book, *Para leer el Pato Donald. Comunicación de masas y colonialismo [How to Read Donald Duck. Imperialist Ideology in the Disney Comic]*, contributed significantly to popularizing in Latin America the imperialist theory of cultural relations between First and Third World countries, in particular the United States and the nations south of its border. Dorfman and Mattelart studied what they perceived to be the capitalist values and behavior imbedded in Disney comic books highly popular in Chile before and during the presidency of Salvador Allende (1970-1973). From an analysis of the comic books' content they extrapolated to the dangers that these seemingly inoffensive stories posed to Chilean children during their formative years. They viewed these values as reflective of the "American dream of life" that the United States imposed upon Third World Countries in order to guarantee its own economic and political survival.

Their underlying thesis of cultural imperialism is now a standard approach for cultural critics who focus on Latin America. A basic tenet of this approach, the role that various popular culture industries—radio, television, photonovels, comic books, advertising, etc.—play within the underdeveloped economies and societies, is derived from the "dependency paradigm," a view of the development process that departs markedly from the more accepted Western models of modernization and development.

While the "modernization paradigm," in vogue among United States social scientists and economic aid policy planners during the late 1950s and early 1960s, focuses on *internal* processes of development and the role of social values, the dependency theory is based on an analysis of the relationship *between* developed and underdeveloped countries. The developmental process and problems of the Third World are examined within the context of these relationships. Accordingly, Third World countries occupy a subordinate position to developed countries in the international economic and political systems. The latter strive to maintain their own process of development at the expense of the developmental needs of the former.

Dependency theorists focus on the relationship between what they identify as the "center" (the developed countries) and the "periphery" (the underdeveloped countries). They see this relationship reproduced in the structure of underdeveloped nations' internal relationships; that is, the polarization between the urban sector, whose interests are often allied and coincide with those of the developed countries (the center), and the rural sector (the periphery), which exists in an exploitative relationship to the urban sector. The role of transnational corporations in dominating the underdeveloped economies is key.

Cultural imperialist theorists such as Herbert I. Schiller focus on these transnational corporations as cultural industries that are essential in shaping a dependent relationship between developed and Third World countries. A primary concern of Schiller revolves around the deleterious cultural consequences that transnational corporations and their domestic counterparts have on Third World societies, especially on the behavior and world view of various audiences.

When we apply the Schiller model—which Dorfman and Mattelart also set forth in their 1972 book—to the *Mexican* comic, we find that what dominates the creation and distribution of this very important Mexican popular culture product is not some monolithic multinational publisher, but several smaller, indigenous and autonomous entrepreneurial companies with virtually no interrelated financial ties. Unlike the Disney comics central to Dorfman and Mattelart's thesis, many of the more popular Mexican comic book titles do *not* reflect the world view of the "center," that is, of the dominant capitalist countries. This is nowhere more apparent than in the image of the United States found in the works of Eduardo del Río (Ríus), and the post-Ríus version of *Los supermachos.*

Ríus' Los supermachos and Los agachados

Eduardo del Río, more popularly known to millions of his readers by his pen name, "Ríus," is unusual among comic book writers in Mexico. He is prolific, versatile, and controversial and was, for many years, the creator of the most explicitly political comic book in his country and perhaps in all of Latin America. Alan Riding, former Bureau Chief for the *New York Times* in Mexico City, calls him a maverick who has set himself apart from other cartoonists by using his comic book form to carry his political message to a mass audience.

In both of his comic books, *Los supermachos* and *Los agachados,* Ríus creates fictitious towns populated by characters representative of various Mexican social types, institutions, and values. While these characters express verbally or through their behaviors a wide range of attitudes and values, they can hardly be seen as constituting a microcosm of Mexican society. For the most part, the characters and settings are rural, as Ríus seems to studiously avoid references to the Mexican urban experience.

On page one of the first number of *Los supermachos,* the author introduces "San Garabato"—it has been suggested that the name derives from a large-sized illegible scrawl or refers to a sharp hook or knife well-known to the Mexican peasant—as a land of "machos, borrachos y compachos" [*"machos,* drunks and buddies"]. He continues, tongue in cheek, that it is a worthless, insignificant town, just like other Mexican towns in terms of the number of *machos* and drunks who live there. San Garabato, however, surpasses others since the *machos-machos [second-rank machos]* have left to become *braceros* [Mexican agricultural workers in the United States] or *mariachis* due to the scarcity of gainful employment.

San Garabato has nothing to distinguish it from most other Mexican towns. The architecture, while typical, is not without appeal: tile-roofed buildings, key-stoned doorways, wrought-iron window grates. While it has a jail and a cemetery, it is evidently too small to have a school. It has no telephones, movie houses, newspapers, soccer or baseball stadium, or restaurants, other than one bar. It is so indistinguishable and so unattractive a town that in the first number a meeting is called by Don Perpetuo to rally the townsfolk to discuss what can be done to attract outsiders, especially *gringos* [American tourists], to bring some money into the community. A unique plan is devised: the town will publicize in Mexico City newspapers that the head of Pancho Villa, one of Mexico's revolutionary heroes, has been discovered in the local cemetery.

Ríus, in Number 30, reiterates how boring and uneventful life is in his fictitious town, and this serves his purpose well: to create a compendium of social, historical, political, and cultural forces that characterize contemporary Mexico. The fact that the setting is rural does not prevent him from introducing problems that plague all Mexicans. The most important components of the population are amply represented. A summary of the various social types represented in San Garabato reveals the possibilities Ríus has allowed himself for presenting the myraid problems— some dating from colonial times, others created by Mexico's rush into industrialization in the twentieth century—which have afflicted Mexican society in the sixties and the seventies.

Juan Calzónzin is the most obvious representative of the twenty percent of Mexico's population which is Indian. While of humble origins and not formally educated, he is nonetheless very astute and philosophically oriented. It has been suggested that perhaps he is the spokesman for Ríus himself. Calzónzin is a Tepuja Indian with no white blood. Through him, Ríus introduces us in a succinct way to the perpetual problem of the Indian as a totally disenfranchised segment of the population that has traditionally been ignored by the government. Don Perpetuo, the local political boss, recommends that Calzónzin try to assimilate himself into civilization. However, he also recommends that his ancestral land should be expropriated. Calzónzin never plays the role of the subjugated downtrodden alien but rather that of an independent assertive individual who is aware of his rights.

Unlike Calzónzin, Chon Prieto is described as a lazy, drunken Indian whose character is more in keeping with the negative stereotype urban upper and middle-class Mexicans have of their country's original inhabitants. Ríus defends his portrayal of Chon as a reflection of the rampant alcoholism which afflicts Mexico's Indians.

Don Perpetuo is perhaps the most extreme stereotype in *Los supermachos*. He is a fat, loud-mouthed *cacique* [rural political boss] who has little tolerance for insubordination or disrespect on the part of any of the townspeople, especially those who are beneath him socially. He wears boots, an absurdly large Western cowboy hat, and dark glasses, and sports a large moustache. Don Perpetuo is generally depicted with his mouth open, shouting orders at the town's policemen and other municipal officials. Significantly, he is often addressed as *führer,* a title that corresponds with his demeanor, his role within the town's political life, and his historical role in Mexican history as a rural regional boss with absolute authority. His office is the bar, his desk the bar counter; it is here that he convenes a meeting to discuss attracting more money into San Garabato. In spite of his awesome power, Ríus allows Don Perpetuo to be dominated by his wife, Doña Pomposa.

Froylán Osorio appears in only the first numbers of *Los supermachos* but long enough for Ríus to ridicule the high airs and pomposity of Mexican intellectuals, especially those dilettantes who make pronouncements on every conceivable subject from Aristotle to Zarathustra. He would appropriately fit the description of the office snob coined by one of our recent Vice-Presidents. Rius takes him to task for refusing to work and for his exclusive "artistic" interest in selling to the highest bidder. Apparently he believes that the essence of poetry is rhyme, for when we meet him he blithely utters: "Acá toy y no me voy" [Here I am, and I'm not leaving"].

Lucas Estornino, a druggist, is a lukewarm politician. He is not very assertive about his ideals, seems intent on pleasing Don Perpetuo, and is more interested in life's comforts than in putting into operation any abstract political ideas.

Arsenio, San Garabato's sheriff, takes orders from Don Perpetuo, always carries them out and never takes any self-initiative. He is thus an ideal public official who is not willing to risk incurring the wrath of his superiors. Lechuzo, his redheaded helper, also is depicted as a faithful lackey of Don Perpetuo. He enforces the "law" with his omnipresent billy club.

Emerenciana, a *beata* [pious woman], embodies all the worst qualities of the perpetually black-robed women whose devotion to the Catholic Church has no equal. Fortunately, Ríus has softened this character with comic elements. Yet she and the other church-going women of *Los supermachos* represent the traditionally conservative character of the Latin American Catholic church.

Don Fiacro Franco represents the *gachupín* [transplanted Spaniard] population in Mexican society. He wears the typical Spaniard's *boina* [beret] and *alparagatas* [hemp sandals] and speaks with the Castilian *zeta*. As discussed earlier, he is a carryover from the political cartoon and most satirists have replaced him with the American businessman. The Franco of *Los supermachos* not only represents this segment of the Mexican population but also obviously refers to the Spanish dictator Francisco Franco, to whom Ríus will later devote a scathing critical number of *Los agachados*.

In Ríus' second comic book, *Los agachados*, he creates another fictitious town, "Chayotitlán," with a complete cast of characters who, in a rough way, resemble the inhabitants of San Garabato: Professor Gumaro, a young leftist intellectual whose observations on politics and society are similar to those of Calzónzin; Don Cefiro, a kind of lower class Sancho Panza whose closest parallel in *Los supermachos* is Chon Prieto; Doña China who, although not a *beata*, voices many of the same concerns as Emerenciana; Yocupicio, the policeman, who functions in Chayotitlán as Estorino does in San Garabato; Don Galileo, an innocent and bumbling shopkeeper; Espiridión, the *campesino;* el licenciado Trastupijes, a more sophisticated version of Don Perpetuo; Don Filipino, a conservative industrialist; an older priest; Doña Tecla, "una mujer decente" ["an upstanding woman"]; Ruquito, a world-wise and drunken old peasant; Lincoro, a fat buffoon; Micaela, a lady who comes back to Chayotitlán after marrying well; and Sr. Diputado, who behaves as arrogantly as Don Perpetuo.

Ríus uses this format as the focal point of interaction between the various representative characters. As in *Los supermachos*, intellectuals threaten the status quo and suffer the consequences; various political, social, and cultural forces clash, citizen's rights are frequently violated, and the lack of education and literacy programs are revealed. In addition, Professor Gumaro, who is more educated and knowledgeable than his counterpart, the naturally wise Calzónzin, uses every pretext to educate his companions through lessons in history, politics and ideology.

Ríus' characterization of the United States is decidedly negative, especially when viewed in its political, economic, and cultural relationships with Mexico. The extent to which Ríus believes that American values (and products) are more acceptable to many Mexicans than their own is depicted on the cover of Number 40 1/2. Calzónzin and Chon are talking to one another. One asks: "¿Y pa qué le gustaria hablar en inglés?" ["Why would you want to speak in English?]. The other answers: "¿Pos en qué país cree que vivimos?" ["Well, in what country do you think we live?"]. This depressing conception of Mexico's sellout to the United States is carried out in other numbers. For example, on the cover of Number 79, Calzónzin is sitting on a rock playing a guitar and singing a lament to the effect that everything in Mexico has always been dominated by foreign interests. The entire number provides a catalogue of U.S. products with which forty million middle-class Mexicans are enamored. Reflecting on exploitive U.S. business interests in Mexico, the wise Calzónzin tells us how the astute American deceives the Mexican by hiring him to work for low wages in plants that they (the Americans) own. The manufactured products are then sold to Mexicans at high prices and the high profits leave the country. The cover of Number 56 shows Calzónzin holding a sign "Gringas sí, Yanquis no," indicating that Mexicans, while welcoming nubile and available American women, have strong feelings against American economic interest in Mexico. Within the pages of this same number, American exploitation comes directly to San Garabato in the form of Meester Rosk— an obvious play on then Secretary of State Dean Rusk—a gangster-type, who establishes a company in the town with the willing cooperation of Don Perpetuo and his side-kick Arsenio who clears the streets of drunks, communists, and ugly and skinny people so that the foreign visitor will not be offended.

Many of Ríus' individual newspaper cartoons depict the United States, symbolized by Uncle Sam, as a manipulator of Mexican government officials and business interests and this view persists in *Los agachados,* his second comic book. The themes of economic and cultural imperialism are found throughout the eight-year duration of the comic book and give unity to the many individual issues in which the United States is referred to. The cover of Number 130 visually depicts this view of the historical relationship between the two countries: Uncle Sam is shown sitting on a toilet which is the map of Mexico. This same issue catalogues the many ways in which Mexico is dominated by its northern neighbor. This is prefaced by what Ríus believes are the three key abuses of Mexico by the United States: 1) a dumping ground for the disposal of its trash: saline water, industrial waste, war-shattered veterans, hippies, drug addicts, and decrepit retirees; 2) a source of abundant cheap labor;

3) a beautiful and inexpensive vacation spot—Ríus comments "if Mexico is a garden, Mexicans are the gardeners."

With his co-author, Herbert Castillo, Ríus in *Huele a gas* [It Smells Like Gas] warns us that we should be aware of the political decisions and other international ramifications that are likely to result from the recent discovery of an abundant supply of oil in Mexico. Of particular concern to Castillo and Ríus is the likelihood that the United States— depicted on the cover as Uncle Sam, who is sniffing the air for the smell of gas—with the complicity of Mexican officials, will deprive the people of their natural resources and, therefore, of the possibility of eradicating hunger, illiteracy, and sickness.

Whether he is dealing with the revolution or the United States' powerful influence on the country's culture and economy, Ríus, in his comic books and illustrated books focuses heavily on Mexico. He is sharply critical of Mexican officials who, because of greed and corruption, allow themselves to be manipulated by foreign interests. The writer deals also with social myths and behavior that he believes are threats to a healthy, dynamic society. But while emphasizing these and other negative aspects of Mexico, Ríus believes that change and progress are possible if modeled after other decent socialist experiments around the world.

The Post-Ríus Los Supermachos

Although several countries such as France, England, Spain, Cuba, and the Soviet Union are described in the pages of the post-Ríus *Los supermachos* as militarists and aggressors, the principal culprit is the United States. Several numbers are devoted to United States imperialism, mainly in Latin America and Mexico, but also in other parts of the world such as South Vietnam. Again, the particular focus of *Los supermachos* is not on the fact that the United States is a capitalist country, but rather on the aggressive exporting of its ideology and economic interests through the overpowering threat of military intervention and other more subtle means.

In the number referred to above in which South Vietnam is depicted as an innocent victim of centuries of foreign domination, the United States emerges as a warmongering world power whose intentions become clear as early as 1965, when this country steps up the construction of military bases and increases the number of troops. *Los supermachos* holds the United States directly accountable for the death of hundreds of thousands of Vietnamese, both military and civilian, and the destruction of large areas of Vietnam through its defoliation campaign. This, coupled with the economic gain derived by large corporations from the sale of arms and herbicides, leads *Los supermachos* to draw a parallel between the United States and the Nazi war crimes revealed as the Nuremburg trials after World War II.

los agachados

de RIUS

la

en méxico !

Tlatelolco,
Díaz Ordaz,
Echeverría..
a la luz del
libro de
PHILIP AGEE

253
$ 2.50

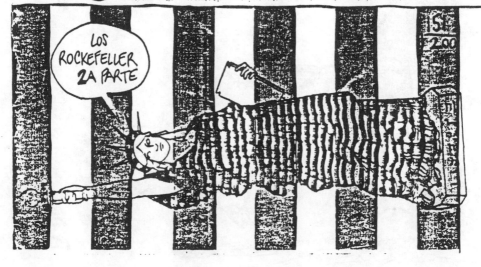

LOS SUPERMACHOS

324001

N-699   AÑO XVII – MAYO 24 DE 1979 – REVISTA SEMANAL $5.00

BRACEROS
INVADEN
E.U.A.

EN ESTE
NUMERO

LAS PREDICCIONES DE KRISHNA THAKUR
DESDE YUGOSLAVIA... CON AMOR

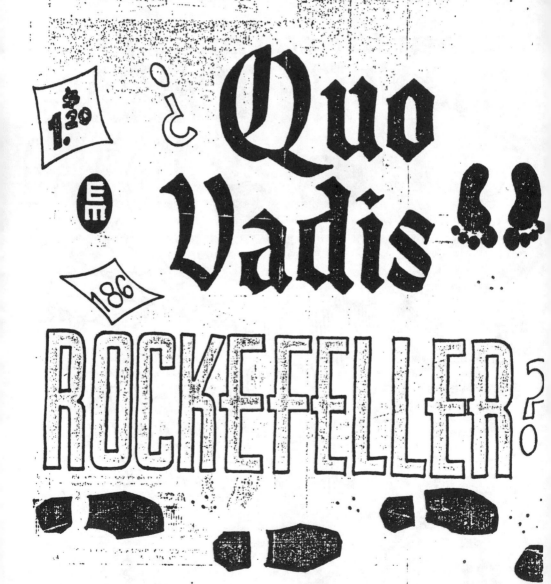

LOS SUPERMACHOS
#200
OPERACION INTERCEPCION
¡NO SEA MENSO!
EM
$1.20

LOS SUPERMACHOS
* VIOLENCIA * SEXO * AGRURAS Y DEMOCRACIA PERO MUY MUY BLANCA *
NÚMERO DEDICADO A LOS NEGROS
FREEDOM NOW!
KKK
..Y CAFÉS CON LECHE QUE LOS ACOMPAÑAN!
Exija con este número un ejemplar GRATIS de
LOS CAMPEONES
una revista que abordará con valor los problemas de nuestro pueblo
90
UN PESO

Los supermachos' overall view of United States foreign policy regarding Latin America is decidedly negative. Many examples of what is interpreted as United States imperialism are cited, including the Monroe Doctrine; the political and economic control of Cuba between 1901 and 1934 under the provisions of the Platt Amendment; the United States-instigated embargo of Cuba late in 1960; the occupation of the Dominican Republic in 1965 by marines; military and spy activities in Nicaragua, Panama, and Guatemala during the last forty years; and the support of the Somoza family dictatorship in Nicaragua.

In several numbers of *Los supermachos,* the related issues of *malinchismo* and foreign economic imperialism in Mexico are addressed. As Malinche cooperated with the Spaniards to betray her own people so, too, have many Mexican leaders through the centuries conspired to sell out the territory, natural resources, and the culture of the Mexican people in exchange for material gain. Santana is seen as the prototype of the *entreguistas* [the "givers"] since he is held responsible for the loss of most of the Southwest and California to the United States. *Entreguismo* enjoyed its Golden Age during the presidency of Porfirio Diaz who allowed foreign investors to take over many of Mexico's most vital industries such as mining, railroads, and utilities.

Los supermachos observes that a whole system of fraud exists that is akin to *entreguismo* and which allows foreign investors to sidestep more recent Mexican laws restricting the operations of foreign corporations: *Los prestanombres* or those Mexicans who front for foreign companies in order to facilitate their proliferation and growth. Chon Prieto has become Mr. Gordon's business associate, and, as Calzonzin explains, this is only part of the American's network of financial holdings in and around San Garabato: Gordon's *latifundios* are in Don Plutarco's name while his mine stock is held for him by Don Perpetuo. In this way, the non-fictitious gringo is able to control business decisions while not being in violation of the Mexican law which stipulates that, in selected industries, fifty-one percent of the corporation's stock must be in the hands of Mexican nationals.

Another problem related to economic imperialism, *malinchismo, entreguismo,* and *prestanombrismo*,* is that brought about by the residence in Mexico of large numbers of Americans whose influence on Mexican culture is severely criticized. Mr. Gordon, the gringo resident of the fictitious town San Garabato, has all the worst stereotypical qualities of Americans: he is gross, materialistic, greedy, culturally

---

*All of these terms refer to Mexicans who sell out their country's national economic interests to foreign enterprises.

insensitive, naive, exploitative, ignorant of the language, racist, suspicious, etc. He is a symbol to the comic book's readers of American culture's most negative qualities.

Soon after arriving in San Garabato, he becomes a dominant figure in the town's economic and social life. He hires Chon Prieto as his *prestanombre*, buys a mine, and invests in several other businesses. In preparation for the arrival of more retired Americans, he has remodeled a local bar which will exclude the townspeople because of their racial background. Even Don Perpetuo will not be allowed to patronize Mr. Gordon's new business, and when he protests to the American that he is the town's mayor, Mr. Gordon reminds him of the salary he pays him to fulfill such a role. Further, Mr. Gordon complains to Don Perpetuo that he is not doing his job, for he has allowed all the Indians—would-be servants for the retired American veterans Mr. Gordon is expecting—to leave San Garabato to become braceros. Don Perpetuo functions on a local level as Mr. Gordon's *entreguista*. He calls a meeting of the residents of San Garabato to convince them of the urgency of preparing the town for the Americans. Although the townspeople protest his efforts to convert San Garabato into a tourist haven, soon more Americans begin to arrive. Like characterization of Mr. Gordon, they are also described as crass and narrow-minded. For example, when Calzónzin mentions the word "death, an American reacts by attacking him with rocks while the Indian recites a litany of United States transgressions—Hiroshima, Nagasaki, Korea, Cuba, Santo Domingo. Calzónzin finally brings the American's attack to an end by simulating an air raid siren, thus taking advantage of his irrational fear of nuclear attack.

Another American national characteristic that is satirized in *Los supermachos* is the paranoid reaction to communism. San Garabato is visited by a harmless Soviet ethnographer interested in collecting scientific data. Mr. Gordon (along with Don Plutarco) reacts with panic, conjuring up visions of hordes of Russians descending upon the helpless San Garabatenos like birds of prey. He offers to call the Pentagon on his hotline to request Army and Navy reinforcements to stop the Russian "invasion" of Latin American.

Los supermachos suggests that the distorted American attitude towards communism has affected certain sectors of the Mexican political establishment, which also has a vested interest in using this fear as a scapegoat for the lack of social progress and opposing (often in a repressive way) individuals and groups in Mexican society who press for change. Don Plutarco, the highest political official in San Garabato and the surrounding region, engages in considerable saber rattling when he learns of the Soviet visitor. Dressed in full Porfirian military dress, he cuts a ridiculous figure, waving his sword and calling San Garabatenos to the barricades to defend the fatherland against the aggressors from the East.

The CIA and the entire United States counterespionage network are singled out in *Los supermachos* for their interference in the internal affairs of foreign countries and their promotion of American values, especially those associated with capitalist business interests; they are seen, therefore, as agents of both cultural and economic imperialism. Mr. Gordon is, again, the perpetrator of CIA plots and the watchdog of American interests in San Garabato. His exaggerated sense of self-importance in this role and the consequences of his resulting myopic vision of reality are satirized. In one number, he is shown in radio contact with an unidentified ally; together, they are tracing a tip that Calzónzin and Don Lucas are hatching a communist plot. He enlists the aid of Don Perpetuo and his secret police—the buffoon Arsenio and his sidekick—to track down the culprits. Mr. Gordon's crisis vanishes into thin air he discovers that Calzónzin and Don Lucas have been installing a window, not plotting to overthrow the government.

On a more serious note, *Los supermachos* untangles for its readers the complex systems, networks, and organizations that comprise United States intelligence. The CIA is highlighted as the one organization that is so feared and hated that even the United States congressmen and other intelligence agencies have called for its dismantling. Its many front organizations and involvements in the affairs of United States organizations and of foreign governments are listed. Among the CIA's various nefarious activities discussed in *Los supermachos* are: the organizing of coups; the psychological manipulation of heads of state and others; political action; intervention against hostile governments through arms, money and troops; and the use of science to achieve questionable political ends. In terms of cultural influence, the CIA finances mass media campaigns to promote American values, attitudes, fashions, music, etc. Reflecting a monolithic conspiratorial interpretation of contemporary events, *Los supermachos* attributes to the CIA the power to mold and control the minds of impressionable young Americans: "Y lo peor, están sembrando en la mente de sus hijos la idea del superhombre yanqui, los invencibles, los todopoderosos, los luchadores por la liberatad y la democracia ["And the worst of it is they are planting in their children's minds the idea that the superhuman Yankee is invincible, all-powerful and the defender of peace and democracy"].

In addition to economic and cultural imperialism, another facet of United States-Mexican relationships dealt with in *Los supermachos* is the treatment of the bracero as well as the related problem of the status of Chicanos in this country. The bracero, or contract-labor program, is viewed as an asset to United States agribusiness but as a hardship on the Mexican worker. One cover of *Los supermachos* makes a succinct statement on the latter. Calzónzin remarks to Chon: "Yo de bracero? Prefiero consumir la explotación, los malos tratos y la discriminación que el país produce" ["Me, a bracero? I would rather accept my own country's exploitation, mistreatment and discrimination"]. Between the covers of this number, he describes his plight from the moment he is contracted in Mexico City to his return after a series of bitter experiences in the United States.

Los supermachos traces how, after losing their land and power to the Americans after 1848, Mexicans, who opted to stay in the United States, very quickly learned that their language, culture, and traditions would not be protected despite the guarantees of the Treaty of Guadalupe Hidalgo. This begins a period during which Chicanos are dominated and treated as racial inferiors. The comic book summarizes their contributions to agriculture, mining, railroads, and cattle raising, that is, to the economic development of the American Southwest and California.

Los supermachos ties increasing Chicano militancy to growing anti-Americanism in Latin America, thus linking patterns of United States imperialism in foreign countries to the oppression of this colonized minority within its own country. In response to a purported call for help from Chicanos, *Los supermachos* devotes a number to discussing their trials and tribulations, the legacy of broken promises, and the determined resistance to continuing domination. Citing the Mexican José Vasconcelos' famous phrase, "Por mi raza hablará el espíritu" ["The spirit will speak for my race"], this number opens with a militant call for all Mexicans to support their Chicano brothers and sisters. It continues by listing the abuses of Chicanos at the hands of an inept and racist police force and Border Patrol, an insensitive educational system, municipal governments who regularly gerrymander voting districts in order to control elections, well-intentioned liberals who do them more harm than good by misrepresenting Chicanos to the American public, and the mass media who systematically distort the news and cast Chicanos in a negative role. In short, *Los supermachos* offers a brief catalogue of institutional racism vis-à-vis Chicanos and makes a case for cultural genocide.

In terms of its treatment of its own minorities and undocumented workers and its "imperialist" posture toward Mexico and other countries, the United States is decidedly cast in a villain's role in *Los supermachos*. To further discredit this country and its values, several numbers are devoted to other negative internal aspects of American culture; crime figures prominently. The comic book characterizes the mafia or *cosa nostra* in this country as a kind of second government, a giant octopus whose tentacles extend into every area of business and government in addition to illegal activities such as drugs, gambling, and prostitution.

This view of gangsterism in the United States has been confirmed in several recent studies. Lawyers, judges, congressmen, the police, and even the Church come under its sphere of influence.

Los supermachos paints a chaotic picture of United States society where violence, drugs, free love, racial strife, and corruption in all realms of public and private life are in full swing, and organized crime is tied vaguely to this general state of demise. Calzónzin's fear that the struggle for power between legitimate and illegitimate forces will spill over into Mexico and other Latin American countries in a way has materialized, given the drug wars that now plague northwestern Mexico. The parallel is drawn between the United States and the decline of the Roman Empire; Mexico, in comparison, is virtually pure, given the limited power of its corrupt *caciques* and police.

While not all Mexican comic books present a negative view of the United States, a case can be made that the titles discussed above portray the Giant to the North as a materialistic, corrupt society intent upon dominating Mexico and the rest of Latin America. These titles pass the cultural imperialism litmus test with flying colors. Collectively they defy the popular belief that all Mexican popular culture industries are controlled by nefarious foreign economic interests. There is no *Pato Donald* to be found here.

Works Cited

Ariel Dorfman and Armand Mattelart, *Para leer el Pato Donald. Communicación de masas y colonialismo* (México, D.F.: Siglo XXI, 1972). This work later appeared in English translation as *How to Read Donald Duck. Imperialist Ideology in the Disney Comic*, trans. David Kunzle (New York: International General, 1975).

Alan Riding. "Maverick Cartoonist Struggles Against Censors," *New York Times* release which appeared in the *Las Cruces* [New Mexico] *Sun-News*, September 13, 1979, Section B, p. 13.

Eduardo del Río (Rius). Eduardo del Rio was the creator, writer and illustrator for *Los supermachos* until 1967 when he left Editorial Meridiano for political reasons. Soon after, he created *Los agachados* which Editorail Posada published from 1968 until 1977. *Huele a gas* (Mexico, D.F.: Editorial Posada, 1977) is one of del Río's over thirty illustrated books.

Herbert I. Schiller. *Mass Communication and American Empire* (New York: Kelly, 1969); *The Mind Managers* (Boston: Beacon Press, 1973); *Communication and Cultural Domination* (White Plains, New York: International Arts and Sciences Press, Inc., 1976).

Los supermachos. After Eduardo del Rio left Editorial Meridiano in 1967, this publisher hired its own writers to write and illustrate their own version of *Los supermachos*. Its characters, setting, etc. legally belonged to Editorial Meridiano.

Part II:
Foreign Uses of American Popular Culture

—*American "film noir": German and Argentine versions*

—*"Playing Indians" seriously in Germany*

—*Confronting Naziism on film in Germany and the U.S.*

—*Rock 'n rollin' against hunger around the world*

UNIVERSITY OF HERTFORDSHIRE LRC

Cat People and Mean Streets: American Popular Film Genres in the Work of Manuel Puig and Wim Wenders

Joan Worley

Filmmakers in the United States did not create either alienation or horror, but American film noir and American horror movies became genres nearly as widely exported as the Western. The range of their influence is reflected in their use during the 1970s and 1980s by Wim Wenders, one of the New German Cinema directors, and Manuel Puig, the experimental Argentinian novelist. Wenders and Puig assume a familiarity with popular film genres on the part of their audiences. Far from serving merely as homage to the artists' favorite old movies, however, the works of Wenders and Puig transform these popular genres into new narrative styles for both fiction and film.

No reader can overlook the fascination with American popular film in the novels of Manuel Puig. Calling Hollywood films "alienated languages," undervalued by their cultures, Puig chooses to make them significant by "putting them at the service of literature" (Christ 58). In *La traición de Rita Hayworth (Betrayed by Rita Hayworth), Boquitas Pintadas (Heartbreak Tango), and The Buenos Aires Affair,* Puig's characters suffer from their attempts to adapt real life to the beautiful illusions of film. Puig's most intense experiment in making the reel real, however, comes in his 1976 novel, *El beso de la mujer araña (Kiss of the Spider Woman).* A blend of dialogue, footnotes, propaganda tracts, and police reports, the novel depends for its momentum on the plots of American B-movies, told by one prisoner to another.

Kiss of the Spider Woman explores the lives of two inmates in a prison near Buenos Aires—Valentin Arreguí, a young revolutionary, and Molina, a middle-aged homosexual whom the warden has offered a parole in exchange for information about Valentin's revolutionary cadre. As in his other novels, Puig experiments with dialogue: much of the book consists of Molina's recitals of the plots of films he has seen. Through such entertainments Molina hopes to gain Valentin's trust, and by this

62

device Puig examines the characters of the men, while simultaneously drawing the contrast between their position in a shabby, confined reality and the freer, magical world of American popular film. The recounting of the film plots gives the novel structure and paces the development of the relationship. The films' content, moreover, serves as comment on the lives of Puig's protagonists. Puig's choice of films is therefore significant: he uses a racing film, a love story, and a melodrama, but given privileged positions within the novel are American horror films.

"—Something a little strange, that's what you notice, that she's not a woman like all the others. She looks fairly young, twenty-five, maybe a little more, petite face, a little catlike." In these first lines of *Kiss of the Spider Woman*, Molina has already begun his retelling of RKO's *Cat People*, the 1942 Val Lewton-Jacques Tourneur thriller, and Puig has begun to establish the structure of the novel as one in which movies vie with reality for authority. Through the next two chapters, which complete both Molina's recital of the film and Puig's introduction of his characters, the significance of Puig's selection of *Cat People* becomes apparent.

When Lewton produced *Cat People* for RKO in the early forties, he hired as director Jacques Tourneur, who was later to make the noir pictures *Berlin Express, Out of the Past,* and *Nightfall*. Tourneur created a noir style in his horror films, emphasizing odd camera angles and distorted sound, as well as the isolation and alienation associated with forties film noir. *Cat People* tells the story of Irena, a woman of Serbian descent, fearful that she carries the ancient curse of a race of cat women who kill their mates when aroused. This fear complicates (and is complicated by) Irena's romance with a young architect, her jealousy of the architect's female coworker, and her treatment by a seductive psychiatrist. Attacks on the coworker and the psychiatrist confirm Irena in her belief, and Irena finally dies a victim of the ancient curse.

Though film noir traditionally has more realistic characters than cat women, Tourneur's style of lighting and setting has the everyday look of film noir rather than the overblown gothic look of more expressionistic horror films. In addition, the dialogue and scenes are matter-of-fact, realistic rather than melodramatic. Most important, the film emphasizes psychological drama over horror—a key noir element. Tourneur seldom shows Irena as the panther, for example, and for a very long time it is possible for the viewer to imagine that her problem is sexual frustration rather than a curse.

For Puig, *Cat People* offers opportunities for playing with the psychology of sexual roles and with the idea of imprisonment. Molina's choice of films underscores the initial difference between the apolitical homosexual and the young revolutionary. Valentin at first reacts with amused condescension, almost contempt, for Molina and his silly film plots, often interrupting Molina with a Marxist reading of the film. Molina's experience of the films is much more direct. He identifies with the heroine, "always with the heroine" (25). Puig's depiction of Molina throughout the novel makes clear that Molina has been victimized by society because of his homosexuality. Thus he naturally identifies with *Cat People's* heroine Irena, trapped in her own frightening sexuality. Valentin sees more of himself in the psychiatrist, though he fails to see the character's imprisonment in his unrelenting rationality. Their reactions to the films continue to reveal the men to each other, though indirectly.

By the same device, the reader comes to know the characters and Puig's themes. On one hand, Puig presents *Cat People* as a Freudian tale of sexual deviance: Irena is to her curse as Molina is to his homosexuality. On the other hand, *Cat People* shows us the victimization, the helplessness, of those whose sexuality is judged to be incorrect by an unyielding society. Using a long running foot note full of Freudian descriptions of the causes of homosexuality—a footnote which treats its human subjects with relentless, dry categorization—Puig refutes an easy Freudian reading and forces the reader to look beyond to the political ramifications of sexual difference.

Valentin and Molina learn to cope with their differences through unending arguments stemming from the films Molina recites. The climax of the plot, and their relationship, comes with Molina's retelling of a zombie film, loosely based on such American thrillers as *White Zombie* and *I walked with a Zombie*. The film involves a young woman come from New York to the Caribbean to take up life with her husband, a widowed sugar planter. Beleaguered by the first wife, now a zombie, and the local witch doctor, the young wife finds herself futilely trying to save her husband's life and ultimately cleansing the island of voodoo.

Molina tells the plot of the film to take Valentin's mind off his misery at having eaten poisoned prison food. During the recital, both Molina and Valentin, now well practiced, are running their own mental movies—Molina's the story of a young patient's love for his tender nurse, and Valentin's a crazed mixture of Catholicism and revolution. These inner films fit the two characters well. The zombie film links more strongly, however, to the plot of *Kiss of the Spider Woman*, in that it mirrors the characters' imprisonment and foreshadows their demise. At first intellect has primacy over emotion in Valentin's mind and Molina lives through emotion to the near exclusion of intellect; as their friendship progresses toward love, emotion surfaces in Valentin and Molina becomes unwillingly politicized. When Molina is released from prison, his love for Valentin becomes a trap: for Valentin's sake, Molina moves zombie-like into the world of radical action, only to be gunned down by his lover's suspicious followers. Such a result suggests that Puig considers the motives behind political action to be based on desire and confusion rather than logic. Valentin, drugged by his captors into a living death, ends up in a morphine dream composed of film clips. The final figure in Valentin's reverie, the Spider Woman ensnared in her own web, combines images of the cat woman and Molina into a figure of terror and sadness.

The stereotypes in American popular films certainly reflect the opinions of the films' time and society, and they may reflect more than viewers choose to see about the political neuroses of an era. Puig, however, seems more intrigued by the possibilities they offer for narrative. Molina's spinning of tales based on films creates a new way for Puig to tell *his* tale, a combination of dialogue, narration and allegory that forces the reader to operate on three levels: the plot of the movie (enormously seductive for the reader as well as for Valentin), the dialogue between the two men (which develops the relationship) and the suggested links between the two men and the films. For this last, the selection of *Cat People* and the old zombie pictures is important, because these two films represent so well the confused sexuality and the entrapment. Their closeness to the prisoners' situation makes them more mesmerizing than the other films Molina tells. *Kiss of the Spider Woman,* however, is neither an ode to old movies nor mere narrative tour-de-force. The layers of tale-telling within tale-telling within tale-telling within tale-telling (Puig telling Molina telling the movies telling stories), represent strongly the thrill of narrative, the magical possibility for a fictional tale to bring together real human beings.

In *Hammett,* West German film director Wim Wenders creates a similar celebration of bygone American genres—hard-boiled fiction and film noir. Dashiell Hammett, often called the originator of the hard-boiled style in fiction, created lean, tough detective heroes in a gritty, realistic world. His equally tough style, spare and distanced, ranged from a laconic and cynical first-person in *Red Harvest* to an even more alienated cinematic third person in *The Maltese Falcon.* John Huston's film version of the *Maltese Falcon,* its dialogue lifted almost whole from the novel, remains the quintessential noir film—dark, brooding, alienated, with tough humor and a tough code. Bogart's performance as Sam Spade personified the hero in both hard-boiled fiction and film noir. In his film adaptation of Joe Gores' novel *Hammett,* Wenders follows a fictional Dashiell Hammett (Frederic Forrest) as he tries to turn his past as a Pinkerton agent into a career as a writer, but is interrupted along the way by a mystery involving his old mentor, James Francis Ryan. Peter Boyle's world-weary Ryan is beyond the crowd in ability but not above corruption. Taking on Ryan's case means a search through San Francisco for Crystal Ling, who weaves a net of false innocence much like Brigid

O'Shaughnessy's web of lies in *The Maltese Falcon*. Sam Spade's angelic secretary, Effie Perine, is replaced in *Hammett* by another sidekick, a well-thumbed librarian (Marilu Henner). The crooked lawyer Hagedorn (Roy Kinnear) recreates in build and style Sidney Greenstreet's Kasper Gutman. David Patrick Kelly parodies Elisha Cook's punks to a nicety, and hard-bitten cops in the mold of *The Maltese Falcon's* Dundy and Pollock dog Hammett's steps.

In keeping with the attempt to recreate characters from *The Maltese Falcon*, Wenders has transformed Gores' original plot. Whereas Gores placed his fictional Hammet in a maze of political corruption, Wenders plays down the political for the personal, sending his Hammett on a quest to establish his own moral code by means of a wild-goose-chase to save a woman already beyond salvation. Thus Wenders has pared down Gores' plot so that it resembles more nearly that of *The Maltese Falcon*. The locales in *Hammett* are specific and familiar to those who have seen American films noir of the forties: the waterfront, the dive, the coldwater flat, the gambling joint, the shadowed streets. They are locales invested with meaning by the earlier genre, for in film noir these places came to represent uncertainty, alienation, isolation and moral relativity. To these settings Wenders adds the noir touches—offbeat high and low camera angles, moody lighting that criss-crosses the sets with shadows, an urgency of pacing that drives the story.

All these details of character, setting, and style make *Hammett* look like a reflection of *The Maltese Falcon* and similar noir films. Wenders goes so far as to use Elisha J. Cook in a minor role, and in the film's lead role Frederic Forrest plays Hammett as though he were imitating Bogart as Sam Spade. Called "Sam" by his friends, Wenders' Hammett takes life with Spade's familiar tense calm, except, of course, for the occasional coughing fit. His speech is as cynically witty as Spade's dialogue, sometimes even a reproduction of Spade's best lines. Spotting Hagedorn's punk on his trail, for example, Hammett corners him at a shoeshine stand, much as Spade confronts Wilmer in the hotel lobby. Later Hammett disarms the gunsel and presents him to Hagedorn, waving the punk's gun and announcing, "A little kid took this away from him, but I made him give it back," (a replica of Spade's "crippled newsie" line in *The Maltese Falcon*). Wenders counts on his audience's familiarity with *The Maltese Falcon*, as he shows by having his fictional Hammett sit down with Hagedorn for an etymological discussion of the real meaning of "gunsel," (the term, which somehow escaped the 1941 censors, for a homosexual boy).

This careful evocation of the earlier genre does not represent, however, the result of mere imitation; instead, Wenders' version of Hammett presents a narrative about narrative, a story about fiction-making, more particularly about the creation of a genre.

Hammett opens with a show-down on the waterfront between two nameless characters played by Peter Boyle and Marilu Henner. This scene fades into a "high-hat" shot from ground level up through the keys of Hammett's typewriter as he works, thus apprising the viewer that the characters in the scene exist only in Hammett's mind and, now, on the page. Though Boyle and Henner are soon assigned their "real" characters as Ryan and the librarian, they, like all the other characters in the film, constantly transform into fictional variations of themselves as Hammett weaves his plots. The blend of reality and illusion is heightened when Hammett falls into the hands of the Chinese crime-boss, Fong. Imprisoned and severely beaten, Hammett cannot be sure which people he sees are real and which are fictional—nor can the viewer. The most fictitious-looking character, an ethereal Chinese girl, materializes to lead Hammett to freedom. The "real" ending of the film, a show-down among Crystal Ling, Ryan, and Hammett, repeats the dialogue of the opening scene and takes place in a spot that exactly duplicates the imaginary setting of that scene.

Hammett, then, is about the birth of a closed world, the American hard-boiled genre with its mean streets, its lean prose, and its ambiguous characters. To represent that world, the German director self-consciously adopts the cinematic style that came from it, recreating the hard-boiled world through the settings, style, and characterizations of film noir.

Wenders does not thereby indulge in an empty celebration of the genre he loves, any more than Puig indulges a taste for "camp" in the use of the horror films. For Wenders, film noir is a source of narrative style even in those works which do not "quote" the genre as does *Hammett*. A case in point is another thriller, *The American Friend*, which is based upon Patricia Highsmith's novel *Ripley's Game*. In this 1977 Wenders film, the highly successful criminal Ripley (Dennis Hopper) fast-talks his terminally ill neighbor Zimmermann (Bruno Ganz) into committing a murder-for-hire in order to leave his family well-off at his death. As murder follows murder, Ripley unwillingly begins to feel concern for Zimmermann, involving himself needlessly in a murder Zimmermann has bungled. Ultimately, however, it is Zimmermann who gives up his life for Ripley, his American friend and the author of his woes.

At first viewing, *The American Friend* looks quite "European" next to the easy familiarity of *Hammett's* shadows and twisted streets. Where *Hammett* has crisp dialogue, *American Friend* has uneasy silences. Where Hammett features recognizable locales shown in economical direction, *American Friend* plays upon ambiguous settings and disorienting jump-cuts, so that even the protagonist's apartment becomes foreign territory. This look, however, is the result of Wenders updating of film noir's basic tenets of corruption, alienation and uncertainty. The narrow, shadowed mean streets become wide open spaces in *The American Friend:*

train stations, metros, highways, hotel lobbies, airports—all the facelessly public spaces indiscriminately duplicated across Europe and the U.S. In Wenders' work they carry the same uneasiness as the dark alleyways of film noir, for they too represent the urban world and its attendant anxieties. Ripley's house (fronted with a portico resembling the White House) is furnished only with a pool table, a juke box, and neon signs, the memorabilia of film noir settings. The Zimmermanns' flat becomes a series of discrete, claustrophobic rooms. This spatial dismemberment illustrates how in Wenders' work the alienation which is at the heart of film noir becomes a pervading sense of disconnectedness. The laconic and aimless dialogue (in English, French, and German) dissociates language from character as well as speaker from speaker.

The same disconnecting process occurs in the editing. The lean quickness of American film noir has been slowed. The pauses that Pauline Kael says you could drive a truck through (Kael 174) show Zimmermann's hesitation and loss of direction. The shadowy maze, the urgency of speech and action so common to film noir have been transmuted into a brightly lit unraveling of all the connections between people and places (even of the psychological webs of film noir) and a corresponding public isolation.

The influence of film noir, then, was at work in Wenders' films before *Hammett*, and it has continued to shape his films since, in spite of his sense of needing to escape being "imperialised" by American film language (Dawson 8). The open emptiness of sunny California becomes as "noir" as the twisted corridors of a house of ill repute in *Paris, Texas*. Seen in this way, *Hammett* becomes not only a celebration of hard-boiled fiction and film noir but also an exercise in breaking free by acknowledging these genres.

In *Kiss of the Spider Woman*, Manuel Puig transforms two American horror films by creating levels of narration. The layering of the original films, Molina's retelling, Valentin's interruptions, and Puig's use of all three envelopes the reader in a complex web of narrative in which it becomes impossible to choose a satisfactory "reality." Similarly, Wenders' *Hammett* presents the reader with "real" characters appearing in fictional scenes in the mind's eye of a fictional version of the real-life author Dashiell Hammett as he spins a plot recognizable as a reflection of the actual plot of a real novel, *The Maltese Falcon*—a tangle which suggests that Hammett is as much a creation as creator of his novels and of film noir. Wenders and Puig emphasize not reality but the power of narrative to create realities. Their works, furthermore, show the enduring power of American popular genres.

Works Cited

Christ, Ronald. "Interview with Manuel Puig." *Partisan Review* 44:1 (1977): 52-61.

Dawson, Jan. *Wim Wenders.* New York: Zoetrope. 1976.
Elley, Derek. *"Hammett." Films and Filming* 338 (November 1982). 24-25.
Kael, Pauline. *The American friend." The New Yorker* 17 Oct. 1977: 174-175.

Cheyennes in the Black Forest:
A Social Drama

Yolanda Broyles González

"Ich habe mit meiner Frau und mit meinen beiden Töchtern—bis die etwa 16 waren—
immer unseren Urlaub verbracht im Teepee im Schwarzwald, im Odenwald oder sonstwo.
Wir haben regelrecht unseren Teepee mitgenommen und echt darin gewohnt, darin
geschlafen. Die Kinder haben Lederkleider gehabt. Die Frau ihr Lederkleid; wir haben
gekocht am Feuer. So ist es gemacht worden und es war wunderschön."
("I always spent vacations with my wife and daughters in our Teepee in the Black Forest—
until my daughters were around sixteen years old. We actually took our teepee with us
and actually slept in it. The children had leather dresses. My wife also a leather dress;
we cooked over an open fire. That's what we did and it was wonderful.")

In the more remote areas of the countryside in the Federal Republic
of Germany it is not uncommon to encounter Indian teepees, hear Indian
drum beats and chants, and see smoke rising from campfires. Tribal
members can be observed going about their business dressed in feather
headdresses, mocassins, and an array of other Native American attire.
The participants in these activities are adult Germans, their families,
and friends who in their free time re-enact Native American traditional
life, including its crafts and dances. They are organized in "clubs"
(Vereine), each named after a different Native American people, but mostly
Plains Indians. They include participants of all generations—usually
entire families—and constitute a serious activity which has been practiced
for more than thirty years. This paper explores this comparative popular
culture phenomenon in an attempt to understand the motivations,
conscious or unconscious, behind this seemingly extreme form of cultural
tranvestitism. This phenomenon cannot be understood without a cross-
cultural or comparative perspective. The transnational power of corporate
industrial capitalism has created what has been called a shrinking world
or global village; the fascination with and emulation of Native Americans
in Germany is but one instance of the Americanization of the global
village, a socio-economic phenomenon we usually identify with items
such as Coca-cola, blue jeans, or transistor radios.

On one level the existence of German "Indians" is a reflection of the age of global communication in which we live. The cultivation of the Indian hobby is made possible by the wide circulation of print media, of film and television images, particularly in the form of U.S. American products—material and ideological—into post-World War II Germany. The ever-growing economic interdependence (or in some cases dependence) among nations has created strong—if even at times oblique—linkages in the areas of mass and popular culture. As the depth of our economic involvement in one another as a total human community intensifies, so does our cross-cultural involvement. The phenomenon of German "Indians" is symptomatic of that involvement in more ways than one. As a study in comparative popular culture the present investigation highlights an area where German and Native American culture seemingly intertwine; and it looks beyond German national boundaries in seeking to understand the dynamics of this phenomenon.

The act of seriously assuming the identity of a wholly different people on a regular basis is not an exclusively German phenomenon. It is practiced in all Central European countries. However, I confine my exploration to the German "Indians," particularly those of the Cheyenne tribe in the Black Forest, where I lived for a decade. During my years there I obtained oral histories from participants. In examining this form of cultural behavior I combine data gained from personal testimony with a consideration of economic class and its influence upon such cultural behavior. I also employ analytical perspectives from symbolic anthropology. The ethnographic approach I adopt to examine these imaginary Indians can shed light on the broader post World War II cultural dynamics of West Germany, of which the German "Indians" form a part.

Important to my analysis is Victor Turner's concept of "social drama," a theory of social conflict which describes tensional eruption between social groups in terms of successive phases of an on-going social process. In Turner's view, some kinds of social conflict share the structure and atmosphere of drama: like drama, social conflict has a "processional form," i.e. it manifests similar describable units, phases, or discreet parts. Turner identifies the four constituent parts of social drama as social breach, crisis, redress, and reintegration.[1] The social drama model—which basically describes a dialectical progression within social processes—provides a useful interpretive framework for exploring cultural phenomena, especially cultural conflict. My thesis is that the phenomenon of German Indians constitutes a form of symbolic action corresponding to the third phase of a social drama described by Turner as the redressive phase. I submit that the German reenactment of Native American life represents a symbolic response to a situation of social breach and crisis within German society.

A German Schism:
The Polarization of Elitekultur/Volkskultur

In seeking to describe the social breach and crisis experienced by various West German cultural sectors, a closer look at contemporary German cultural schisms and of the German Indians' positioning within that societal schism is essential. In other words, we must look beyond acts of leisure-time activity to the dynamics of daily social life in order to better understand the burning desire of some Germans to spend their free time in a teepee.

From my interviews with members of the German Cheyenne tribe two significant facts concerning their daily social life emerged. One is linguistic, the other a reality of economic class—and both are related. In the initial phase of these interviews, interviewees began (symptomatically) by speaking New High German of sorts, but invariably switched within minutes to their native tongue, *Allemanisch,* the language of the Southwest corner of Germany and adjoining portions of Switzerland and France. Clearly, they did not feel comfortable with the official German national language, which is not what they speak with their family and friends. These are in fact first-generation speakers of New High German, and they avoid it whenever possible.

Another significant fact is that the overwhelming majority of German Cheyennes are blue-collar laborers whose families in recent years have had to abandon their traditional rural or village societites. They work in factories, on construction sites, as garbage collectors. They are persons who, on the one hand, have experienced a socio-economic uprooting, yet have not made (nor will they necessarily ever make) the cultural transition into the hegemonic transnational *Einheitskultur* that in the Federal Republic of Germany is promoted by the culture industries, educational institutions, and the government. Members of traditional cultures have partially managed to resist the cultural homogenization measures intended to promote the interests of nationhood and of an ascendant bourgeoisie. More recently they have to some extent resisted the growing onslaught of worldwide economic hegemony and the resultant standardization of taste evidenced by the foothold of Coca-cola, Blue Jeans, Hollywood films and other American mass media. Although participation in the official language and culture of German nationhood as well as in the transnational corporate culture is to some degree inevitable, various sectors of traditionalist regional culture in Germany have shown a high degree of resilience. Youths who have had to abandon their homelands in search of work, usually identify culturally and psychologically with their place of origin and not their work locale.[2] Yet from the perspective of mainstream media and governmental hegemony, these native regional cultures have come to be considered marginal.

Such marginalization or, alternately, absorption of distinctly regional cultures, is in no way peculiar to the Black Forest and its native inhabitants, but characteristic of post World War II German society as a whole. In fact, the considerable socio-cultural disruptions caused by the war itself have been matched by those effected by the peacetime Marshall Plan for Economic Recovery and by Germany's eventual junior-partner status in the capitalist bloc headed by the United States. Marked social-cultural change is a process that began at the turn of the century but rapidly accelerated after World War II. The power of transnational corporations and their destructive impact upon indigenous cultures has often been analyzed with regard to Third World nations, but their effects upon indigenous cultures in the industrial nations themselves are sometimes overlooked.

Postwar Germany has seen a process of radical change involving large-scale industrialism (requiring a highly mobile labor pool), accelerated urbanization, and the establishment of multiple mass communications media. All of these factors have brought about a decisive shift from a predominantly village-centered/agriculturalist/regionalist German folk society to a labor-dependent, pan-German corporate industrial society. The fundamental cultural schism that has resulted is that between a cultural elite centered upon print culture and the indigenous oral folk cultures. (Of course, other kinds of schisms, which I cannot discuss here, have also occured. Nor are the existing cultural camps uninfluenced by each other.) What I seek to illustrate here, however, is that the accelerated uprooting process and socio-cultural disruption since World War II have created a distintegration of traditional communities and an attendant human crisis largely unacknowledged or questioned because it is held to be justified by the ends of the modern German economic "miracle" *(Wirtschaftwunder)*. Yet, whereas the *Wirtschaftwunder* has absorbed many Germans and created highly visible economic and cultural elites, those who have not been acculturated, linguistically or otherwise, suffer the effects of marginalization. On a daily basis, members of distinct regional cultures experience pressure to adapt to the new social order applied with great psychological authority by the mass media and by educational agencies, both of which represent hegemonic elite culture.

The German Cheyennes in their everyday social lives occupy a position separate and apart from elite culture. For example, in Germany language is a prime indicator of that cultural schism. The attempted marginalization of dialect speakers (conscious or unconscious) is evident in the typical reactions of New High German speakers when an individual speaks dialect in their presence, or even when an individual speaks New

High German with strong traces of a non-High German mother tongue. Such reactions of non-dialect speakers range from distanced bemusement or polite embarrassment to active expression of contempt. While in Germany I noted, for example, that what many middle-class New High German speakers found annoying about ultra-conservative Social Democrat Party leader Franz Joseph StrauB is the Bavarian dialectal coloring of his speech and not necessarily his politics. Particularly at centers of governmental power, such as administrative agencies or schools, speakers of Germany's numerous native tongues face considerable difficulties as they attempt to maneuver in New High German—a foreign language for most Germans. Unlike Switzerland, whose regional dialects have become official languages, West Germany has opted for a program of tacit annihilation. As in many parts of the world, an official hegemonic language (usually the print culture version of a formerly oral dialect) is made to serve the interests of nationhood and of the current economic order. The gradual annihilation of the regional native tongues of course has signified the erosion of folklife in general, specifically of the rich *oral* cultures transmitted through the ages in regional tongues. The class-based myopia and attendant misperception and disregard vis-a-vis the native oral culture is also evidenced in the frequent identification of oral culture with the print-culture-based negative concept of "illiteracy." That hegemonic perception of oral culture is even shared by many German ethnographers who considered themselves specialists in matters pertaining to regional cultures. Ethnographer Hermann Bausinger, for example, espouses this hegemonic print culture vision of Germany's native tongues: "Whoever complains about the erosion of the good old dialects, should actually also join in the complaint over the end of illiteracy."[3]

The steady uprooting of regional cultures, the erosion of their economic base (in farming and traditional trades) constitute a social breach which has escalated into a human crisis involving virtually all of Germany's cultural regions. The minority or underdog status of those rooted in a regional indigenous German culture obviously represents a historical reversal or social breach, leading to a protracted crisis situation in which the native ultimately comes to be considered the alien. Victor Turner, in his book *Dramas, Fields, and Metaphors* indicates that in a protracted crisis situation such as the one I have described "there is a tendency for the breach to widen and extend until it becomes coextensive with some dominant cleavage in the widest set of relevant social relations to which the conflicting or antagonistic parties belong."[4] The dominant cultural cleavage or crisis I have described here constitutes a reality of which dialect speakers in contemporary Germany are keenly aware, particularly those who are working class. In their condition of "otherness" they occupy—culturally and economically—an underdog position shared by other groups such as so-called *"Gastarbeiter"* (foreign workers) or the *Sinti,* or so-called "gypsies. It is a state of perpetual crisis of identity, a state of continual tension between the forces of assimilation and the human impulse toward cultural self-preservation and self-determination.

Black Forest Cheyennes as Symbolic Action

At this point I wish to address the Black Forest Cheyennes more directly and elaborate upon how their transvestite activity can be interpreted as a type of "redressive action" within the social drama of Postwar German cultural transformations. Victor Turner describes "redressive action" as the third phase of a social drama which typically follows the stage of breach and crisis. This third phase typically limits the spread of crisis through certain adjustive mechanisms. Redress consists of measures taken or acts performed in order to minimize or eliminate tension within a disturbed social system. In his discussion of "redressive mechanisms" Turner says of such mechanisms: "They may range from personal advice and informal mediation or arbitration to formal juridicial and legal machinery...to the performance of public ritual."[5] Of particular interest is the close relationship Turner establishes between the concepts of "redress" and "symbolic action":

It is in the redressive phase that both pragmatic techniques and symbolic action reach their fullest expression....Redress (too) has its liminal features, its being 'betwixt and between' and, as such, furnishes a distanced replication and critique of the events leading up to and composing the "crisis."[6]

Turner indicates how states of what he calls *communitas* or "liminality" often emerge in the redressive phase of social dramas. Communitas is a state of group cohesiveness which temporarily suspends or transcends the everyday social forces which govern society.[7] The states of communitas or "liminality," often characteristic of the redressive phase of a social drama involve a suspension of the everyday pragmatic activity of the real world. The redressive phase can entail a ritual, a trial, or a retreat. What is most significant is that the activity in the state of liminality during a redressive phase stands in symbolic relationship to the breach and crisis phase of the social drama. In other words, the redressive phase of social drama triggers a proliferation of symbolic activity or a "distanced replication" (Turner) of elements from the social crisis. Turner indicates that "this replication may be in the rational idiom of a judicial process, or in the metaphorical and symbolic idiom of a ritual process...."[8]

The phenomenon of the German Cheyennes constitutes a form of redressive behavior, however, significantly, it is not necessarily of the kind that brings about a resolution of the crisis, but only a partial escape from that social conflict. I suggest that the avid re-enactment of a foreign (i.e. American Indian) culture constitutes a metaphorized expression of the cultural marginalization I have described above. It seems significant that the Black Forest natives have chosen to assume the roles of Native Americans, peoples whose history is synonymous with cultural and physical marginalization at the hands of a hegemonic central authority and its agents. Is this tragedy of human history what the indigenous inhabitants of the Black Forest identify with?

To answer this question I must digress briefly and acknowledge that a strong fascination with American Indians is a fact of German life in general. It applies to all Germans from all walks of life and all age groups. *All* German adults I have consulted on the topic (individuals born since the turn of the century) claim to have played Indians as children. After the second World War the cowboy also entered the scene and the game became one of cowboys and Indians. Yet it was the role of the Indian that was always the most coveted. Such massive identification with Native Americans predates the postwar influx of Hollywood versions of the myth of the Wild West.

The vast German fascination with Indians in fact can be traced back to the writer Karl May (1842-1912), the most widely read German author of all time.[9] His Indianist children's books have been widely read by at least three generations of Germans. Karl May in turn can be seen as one manifestation within a broader context of Indianist literature which left its mark upon him and other Germans. Native Americans enjoyed great vogue in early 19th-century American literature, especially among writers such as James Fenimore Cooper, Washington Irving, and Susanna Rowson.[10] The vast majority of Karl May's 65 published titles, which have sold an estimated 55 million volumes, contributed significantly to the creation of an idealized and romantic Native American stereotype in Germany.[11] Interestingly, during his lifetime Karl May at times dressed in the attire of various of the foreign protagonists of his novels, and circulated photos of himself dressed in costume. Since 1952 May's works have been filmed as well as dramatized and performed on a regular basis both in Bad Segeberg (Schleswig-Holstein) and Elspe (Sauerland). The Karl May Society in Hamburg (membership: 700) dedicates itself to researching the life and work of the author.

In addition to the mass interest in Native Americans evidenced through the inordinate popularity of Karl May, an extraordinary interest in Native American culture is also manifest at the academic level: German ethnographers were among the first and most outstanding researchers of Meso-American cultures. The work of ethnographers such as Krickeberg, Seler, or Lehmann ranks among the definitive works on Meso-America. It is a curious fact that German Indians, who are people from an oral culture, have assimilated information on Indians mainly through the vehicle of print culture. One of the German Indian elders describes the struggle to obtain published materials pertaining to Native Americans during the post-war era in contrast with today. Interestingly, he never mentions the film medium as a source of inspiration or information:

Die ersten Bücher, die ich in die Hand bekam, waren die Serien von Fritz Steuben. Das ist was mir in Erinnerung ist. Und dann war es in der Zeit—die frühen fünfziger Jahre—sehr schwierig überhaupt etwas besseres zu kriegen an Literatur, nicht? Deutsche Übersetzungen von guten ethnographisch—fundierten Werken oder Reiseberichten kamen erst viel viel später. Von der Vorkriegzeit gab es auch einiges, aber in den Nachkriegsjahren war es nicht möglich in Deutschland so was zu kriegen. Wo es dann ging, hat man angefangen aus Amerika sich etwas zu bestellen. Das war dann vorwiegend englische Literatur, und wir konnten mit englischer Literatur noch nicht arg viel anfangen. In der Zwischenzeit gibt es da fast jede Möglichkeit an Quellen oder Material. Ich bin seit 1970 jedes Jahr drüben gewesen. Hab' sehr viele Freunde unter den Indianern gefunden. Bin in der Zwischenzeit adoptiert von einer Indianer Familie.*

("The first books I got my hands on was the series written by Fritz Steuben. I remember that. And during that time—the early fifties—it was very difficult to get any decent publications. The German translations of good ethnographically sound works or travel literature didn't appear until much later. There were some things from before the war; but in post-war Germany it was not possible to obtain such. We started to order things from the United States whenever possible. Those things were of course for the most part written in English; and we were at a loss with things written in the English language. Nowadays there are all sorts of possibilities when it comes to sources or materials. And I have gone to the United States every year since 1970. I've found many friends among the Indians; and I've even been adopted by an Indian family.")

In spite of the enduring tradition of German fascination with Native Americans, the response to groups like the Black Forest Cheyennes from other German citizens nonetheless tends to be derisive and condescending. In the eyes of those middle-class Germans I questioned, this form of cross-dressing—performed by all during childhood—is viewed askance when practiced by adults. A few quotes from interviews for the sake of illustration:

"Das sind erwachsene Kinder" ("Those are adult children.")—German professor.
"Die Deutschen haben schon immer alles sehr gut nachgemacht" ("Germans have always been great imitators.")—a sociologist
"Ach das ist bloss romantischer folklore-Kitsch" ("All this stuff is just folkloric kitsch.")—grade-school teacher.

*All translations are mine. First from Allemanisch into New High German: then from New High German to English. Instead of attempting to render the original Allemanisch—an oral tongue and culture which I am unable to adequately transcribe—I decided to present quotations in 'Schriftdeutsch' (written German language). Although I do consider the omission of the original a hegemonic act I decided in favor of New High German in order to secure a wider readership.

"Das ist die Suche nach der Realisierung eines Ideal-Ichs. Sie haben verschiedenste Bilder aus verschiedensten Klischeevorstellungen und Größenphantasien internalisiert. Da gibt es auch eine regressive Ebene." ("This represents the search for the realization of an ego-ideal. They have internalized numerous images from various chiché phantasies and delusions of grandeur. There is a regressive level to all of this as well.")—a psychoanalyst.
"Vereinsmeierei" ("The bandwagon effect.")—a teenager.

In coming to an understanding of what the attraction of Native Americans is for the Black Forest Cheyennes, their own testimony is revealing. To begin with, all of them are quick to distance themselves from the author Karl May, indicating that his works are a terrible distortion of Native American reality. One German Cheyenne teenager indicates:

Der Karl May hat so Bücher geschrieben:*Winnetou* und so. Das können wir auch vergessen. Das ist ja nichts, gel? Das entspricht nicht der Realität. Durch das Lesen von Indianer Büchern ist mein Interesse wach geworden. Das entwickelt sich mit der Zeit. Man kommt auf Bücher, liest sie. Aber Karl May: das ist nichts; das kann man in der Keller tragen.

("Karl May wrote some books: *Winnetou* and such. But we can forget about that. Those books don't really amount to much. They do not correspond to reality. My interest in Indians came alive by reading books about Indians. It developed with time; one comes across books about Indians. It developed with time; one comes across books, reads them. But Karl May—he certainly doesn't amount to much. You can take those books and put them in the basement.")

The German Cheyennes refer much more positively and most frequently to the Indian novels of Fritz Steuben (1898—?).[12] Why they do so may be suggested by the following characteristic passage translated from the preference of one of his best known titles *Der fliegende Pfeil (Flying Arrow)* 1930:

Just imagine if, during the time around the birth of Christ, people had invaded old Germania; people outfitted with all the weapons of civilization; people full of brutality and hypocrisy, which often distinguishes the so-called civilized when they come up against weaker people with a smaller population; people who form alliances around family ties, clans and tribes.

Furthermore imagine that the invaded country was ten or twenty times the size of Germany. Now you can imagine the situation that the Indians of North America saw themselves confronted with.

Those Indians are comparable to the old Germanic tribes. Of course, the Indians were not yet familiar with the use and processing of metals, but they certainly lived like the Germanic tribes in protected villages and they sustained themselves from hunting and fishing. They knew how to plant things, even if not in the same measure as the Germanic tribes. They were a people of the forest; they were open-hearted, hospitable, brave and freedom-loving. They exercised blood-revenge. In their battles they were certainly less restrained and more blood-thirsty than the Germanic tribes. But they had more reason to be that way. For 200 years the Indians struggled against the white invaders. The redskins were betrayed, robbed and plundered a thousand times...The white man had the power.[13]

It is significant that Steuben perceives so many parallels between the vanished Germanic tribes and the American Indian. Although a certain idealization is observable in his text, it is still an analysis of considerable validity in its depiction of power relations, of the white invasion, of a life-and-death struggle for survival. In today's Germany, the German Indians could be said to occupy the position of the subordinate Indian, even though they have not experienced physical genocide.

The oral testimony of the German Cheyennes, quite independently of references to Fritz Steuben, strongly affirms their attitudes of sympathy and identification with a people who have suffered and continue to suffer. As one respondent commented, "My interest has grown from a love for these people who have had to suffer so much. I always read the *Akwesasne Notes*. My interest also developed through novels. And through that feeling of 'This can't possibly be true; this has got to be wrong.' Then I sought out good literature. We also visit the museums; we look at things ourselves" ("Das Interesse entwickelt sich aus Liebe zu diesem Volk, was so viel leiden muβte. Ich lese immer die *Akwesasne Notes*. Mein Interesse kam auch durch Romane. Und dann das Gefühl 'Das kann doch nicht die Wahrheit sein; das kann doch nicht stimmen' Dann fand ich gute Literatur. Wir gehen auch in die Museen, wir gucken uns die Stücke an.") Another youth comments concerning his identification with Indians: "Ich kann für mich sagen, wenn ich irgendwas herstelle—indianische Arbeit—dann geschieht es, weil ich mich identifiziere mit dem Indianer." ("For myself I can say that whenever I produce an object—an Indian artifact—I do so because I identify with the Indian.") Some tribal members variously expressed a consciousness of perhaps being viewed as peculiar, yet persisting in what they consider a life-enriching activity:

Ich müβte der Ehrlichkeit halber sagen, dab dies natürlich schon ein kurioses Hobby ist. Ich würde es zum Beispiel auch komisch finden wenn ich jetzt in ein Indianer-Reservation in Karlsbad käme, und da würden also die Indianer mit Lederhosen und bayrischem oder tiroler Hut sich zeigen. Das würde mir wahrscheinlich auch irgendwie lächerlich vorkommen. So muβ man den Leuten zugestehen, daβ die was wir machen auch irgendwo lächerlich finden. Aber wenn man da mal vielleicht mit so Leuten - also Nicht- Eingeweihten - gesprochen hat, dann wird es vielleicht klarer was wir suchen oder zu finden glauben.
("In all honesty I do have to say that this is naturally a somewhat strange hobby. I would of course also find it strange if I were to arrive in an Indian Reservation in Carlsbad and find the Indians running round with Lederhosen and a Bavarian oder Tyrolean hat. That would probably strike me as being ridiculous. And so we must allow for the fact that some people might well consider what we do ridiculous. But if one perhaps speaks with such people—the uninitiated—then they might understand what we seek or believe to find [by imitating Indians].")

Contrary to popular opinion, romantization or idealization of the Native American people is not foremost in the attitudes of the German Cheyennes. They are aware of the problems faced by American Indians, such as alcoholism on the reservations, poverty, unemployment, and governmental efforts to displace Indians once natural resources have been discovered. There is an understanding of Native American history. One German Cheyenne draws a comparison between reservations and concentration camps:

Ich habe immer gesagt, daB die Indianer-Reservate die ersten Konzentrationslager waren. Wo sie die Indianer eingesperrt haben in Oklahoma: sie haben sie zusammengepfercht mit dem Ziel sie so schnell wie möglich aussterben zu lassen. Die Cheyennes sind auch damals dezimiert wordern bis zum letzten. Manche sind jedoch ausgebrochen und sind hoch, haben den Marsch gemacht durch ganz Mittelamerika durch. Und dauernd verfolgt von den Soldaten.
("I've always maintained that the Indian reservations were the first concentration camps. When they locked up the Indians in Oklahoma they rounded them up with the goal of having them die off as quickly as possible. The Cheyennes were also decimated at the time, down to almost the very last person. Yet some of them escaped and made their way north, they marched through the entire central portion of the United States. And they were constantly pursued by soldiers.")

Their hobby involves a process of constant education concerning American Indian life and much hard work in learning and practicing the traditional crafts, such as the treatment of hides. One tribal member describes the painstaking appropriation process involved in learning traditional Native American crafts:

Da gibt es unwahrscheinlich viel Material. Auch von den Museen haben wir gelernt: in Berlin, in Stuttgart, in Zürich. Aus diesen Sammlungen. Da gibt es gute Sachen. Nicht genau kopiert; oft ein biBchen abweichend. Aber so gut als möglich wird's gemacht. Ich habe meinen Teepee selbst gemacht.
("There is an incredible amount of material [from which we learn]. We have also learned from the museums: in Berlin in Stuttgart, in Zürich. From all those collections. Good things can be found there. We don't copy them exactly; sometimes there is a little bit of deviance. But we construct it as best we possibly can. I made my own teepee.")

An older man indicates: "I am familiar with virtually all existing writings on Native Americans. I have visited all the museums there are— in order to take photographs, in order to learn how something is made." ("Ich kenne ziemlich alle Literatur, die es gibt. Ich habe alle Museen besucht, die es gibt—um zu fotographieren, um etwas dort abzusehen.")

A second factor linking the German Cheyennes with Indian life is the environmental ethic which they share, the ties that bind humans, the earth, the elements and the cosmos. Fundamental to the practice of tribal life and of an environmental ethic is access to land which the tribe leases from a village. In the words of one tribal member:

Man muß einen Platz haben um das Teepee aufzustellen oder das Lagerfeuer zu machen und die Gesänge zu machen, oder die Arbeiten zu machen. Irgendwie setzt dieses Hobby voraus, daß ein Platz, der sich eignet, vorhanden ist. Ich kann in der Großstadt in einem Hochhaus das nicht machen. Da ist die Atmosphäre nicht da. Geistig geht das vielleicht noch. Aber eigentlich paßt das nicht. Ich muß den Boden fuehlen. Ich muß nass frieren; ich muß schwitzen am Tag. Die Temperaturunterschiede machen mir gar nichts aus. Man kann dieses Hobby nicht am Stammtisch betreiben.

("One has to have a place to put up teepees or to build a fire or to perform the chants or to do the crafts. This hobby presupposes that one has a place [land] which is suitable, which is available. I can't do all this in the city in my high-rise apartment. Mentally perhaps. But actually it really has no place there. I need to feel the earth. I need to feel the damp cold and to sweat during the day. I don't mind the daily fluctuation in temperature at all. This hobby can't be performed at the Stammtisch [in a bar].")

The tribe shares the outdoor life on that leased plot of land adjacent to a mountainside, and all available free time is spent in teepees. Their strong attachment to this shared activity is evident in the fervor of their testimony. One elderly man who has enjoyed such tribal life since 1950 reports:

Wir haben auch viel junge Leute im Klub, nicht? Es sind nicht alle alte Leute wie ich. Aber die Älteren können nicht mehr so wie sie wollen, wenn sie älter sind. Ich glaube das geht nicht mehr so mit dem Schlafen. Ich schlafe hier auf dem Bisonfell und fühle mich ganz wohl dabei. Auch meine Kollegin.

("There are plenty of young people in the club, you know. Not all are old people like me. But the older ones can't do everything they'd like to do. Some of them have trouble sleeping out here, for example. I sleep here on this buffalo skin and feel really great doing that. So does my companion.")

A young tribal member similarly relishes the tribal outdoors:

Ich muß arbeiten, um meine Familie zu ernähren. Ich würde lieber in meinem Teepee wohnen. Aber es geht nicht. Aber dennoch stellen wir unsere Teepees hier auf. Die Woche durch arbeiten wir und am Wochenende leben wir im Teepee, auch in den Ferien. Das ist schöner als in meinem Schlafzimmer.

("I have to work in order to feed my family. Of course I would prefer to live in my teepee. But that is not possible. But still we set up our teepees here. We work the whole week through but during the weekend and on our vacations we live in teepees. It's more beautiful there than in my bedroom.")

Some would indeed prefer to leave civilization entirely:

Ich baue meinen Teepee auf und lasse es im Sommer manchmal vier Wochen stehen. Wenn ich dann zur Arbeit gehe und dann am Wochenende frei habe, dann gehe ich wieder in den Teepee. Jeder muB seiner Arbeit nachgehen. Wenn man Rentner wäre, wäre es wunderschön! Ich ginge in den Schwarzwald hoch, oder wo, mit dem Teepee.

("I put up my teepee in this place during summer vacation leave it standing for four weeks at a time. When I return to work and have the weekends off I return to the teepee. We all have to work at our jobs. How wonderful it would be to be retired! I would simply take off with my teepee high into the Black Forest, or wherever...")

An integral part of tribal life is the networking that goes on across tribes. Forms of community building include mutual visiting among tribes as well as trips taken in common. The highlight of each year is the big inter-tribal powwow held during the Whitsun holidays. Such gatherings attract—according to tribal member testimony—a minimum of two-thousand participants from all over Germany and adjoining European countries.

In addition to such testimony, the seriousness and perseverance with which Native American life is re-enacted point to a symbolic affinity between the lives and historic experience of members of German *Volkskulturen* and Native American culture and experience. It is the drama of one marginalized people giving expression to that marginalization by re-enacting the experience of another marginalized and subordinate people. The Germans' reenactment of the Cheyennes offers a "distanced replication" of their own status in greater society and represents, as such, a symbolic action.

At the same time this re-enactment of a foreign culture allows for a complete if even only temporary withdrawal from a society in which the everyday is marginalization and 'being yourself' is a highly conflict-laden enterprise. Instead of freely cultivating their own German traditional cultural practices which have increasingly—especially among youth—become a mark of shame, individuals choose to escape from "Germanhood" altogether by assuming the identity of a foreign people idealized since childhood. Where the struggle against cultural and economic hegemony does not appear a realistic choice, members of Germany's regional cultures adopt the guise of those who did struggle. The withdrawal into the sheltered environment of Native American identity signals at once a denial of the current social structure associated with "being German" and an element of wish-fulfillment fantasy. Through the meticulous cultivation of handcrafts and practice of an environmental ethic, the German Indians turn their backs upon corporate capitalism, its modernity, its conspicuous consumerism. Indian activity takes place almost in the naked state: "Im Sommer tragen wir fast gar nichts. Nur eine Schürz und Mocassins. Man trägt das Nötigste was man braucht. Alles andere ist Ballast." ("During the summer we wear almost nothing at all. Only a loincloth and mocassins. We wear only a bare minimum, what we absolutely need. Everything else is ballast.") The Indian hobby, which unites persons from all generations, also affirms traditional community. In this symbolic sheltered state of Indianhood Germans are able to affirm traditional cultural values yet—significantly— not their *own* (except linguistically speaking). In a society where cultural displacement is becoming the norm, playing Indians provides a self-elected and demonstrative means of not being yourself.

German Indianhood, Punkdom, or other extreme cultural trends might well be understood as cultural responses to the same gap created by the cultural displacement and attendant cultural standardization of postwar Germany. The German Cheyennes place themselves in "liminality," a condition outside or on the peripheries of everyday life, through self-alienation, by assuming the role of an alien. They provide a distanced replication of their real life marginalization (eccentricity) by assuming an eccentric identity and performing eccentric rituals. Thus they exhibit the redressive phase of a social drama, yet with no *redress*— only re-dress or transvestitism. Clothing across customary lines (i.e. as Indians) would appear to give metaphorical expression to a subordinate position by re-enacting that of another subordinate people. Yet that expression is confined to a metaphorical and separatist state.

Pragmatic redressive action by marginalized members of German *Volkskulturen* has to date been minimal in the Federal Republic of Germany, especially when compared to the Basque regionalist opposition in Spain or to the Occitanian movement in France, both of which are directed against the hegemonic powers of a central authority. The reality of cultural marginalization of indigenous populations in all parts of Germany is not prominent in public cultural discourse, a discourse whose *lingua franca* is, of course, New High German, not the regional dialects, and whose medium is print culture, not the oral culture of the *Volkskulturen*.

The minimal opposition to the often subtle but pervasive influence of corporate industrial culture and to institutions of German elite culture is perhaps due in part to the more even distribution of wealth in Germany. The fact that all economic classes of Germans have benefited materially from postwar corporate industrialism may dull the pain of cultural marginalization for many. On another level, the failure to actively seek protection for regional cultures and to openly militate for their cultivation in Germany is related to the identification of *Volkskulturen* or even the term *Volk* with the National Socialism of the Hitler era. The extent to which such a sweeping identification (established by postwar intelligensia) is at all fair cannot be decided here. Whether justified or not, that reality also serves as a barrier to any defense—or even discussion— of the state of German *Volkskulturen*. Organizing as *Allemannen*

(Alemannic peoples) in the Black Forest (instead of in the symbolic form of Indians) would most certainly elicit even greater derision, in addition to being politically suspect.

The conflict situation created by an increased hegemonic marginalization and/or extinction of Germany's indigenous regional cultures continues without appreciable resistance. As Victor Turner points out, not every social drama reaches a clear resolution, particularly when the parties involved are of unequal strength. Turner envisions such crisis relationships between a weak, disturbed community and a powerful central authority "a matter of endemic, pervasive, smoldering factionalism, without sharp, overt confrontation between consistently distinct parties."[14] Interestingly, such tension has become overt in the Black Forest only in conjunction with other issues. The highly publicized struggle between indigenous sectors (in particular the peasantry) of Baden-Württemberg and the state and federal governments over the nuclear reactor site Wyhl (near Freiburg) during the 70s triggered something of a renewed cultural consciousness among some sectors of the Alemannic peoples. Indeed, much of the popular rebellion was conducted in the region's native tongue, utilizing traditional songs, sayings, etc. German Indians of the Cheyenne tribe, however, are far from offering active resistance. Yet within the semantic system of 'being German' their adoption of Indianhood constitutes a powerful non-verbal human metaphor of iconoclasm.

We cannot predict the outcome of this social drama. In Turner's estimation, the third phase (redressive phase) is followed by "either reintegration of the disturbed social group or of the social recognition and legitimization of irreparable schism..."[15] Given the complexity of social relations in the Federal Republic of Germany and the multiplicity of political issues and problems, it is impossible to know how situations of the kind treated here might be addressed. History will witness whether the German Cheyenne's symbolic affirmation of otherness will become a truly redressive movement or whether it will remain a symbolic form of redress.

Notes

[1]This model of socio-cultural conflict is discussed in Victor Turner, *Dramas, Fields, and Metaphors* (Ithaca & London: Cornell University Press, 1974), especially Chapter One, "Social Dramas and Ritual Metaphors."

[2]This fact had been borne out not only in the oral histories I have collected with members of the German Cheyenne tribe in the Black Forest but also in a separate set of oral histories I conducted with the youth of small town in the German Eifel (Palmersheim/Kreis Euskirchen) in the years between 1975 and 1985. The two generations born since World War II have had to learn New High German and

to leave Palmersheim in order to earn a living within the new economic order, one which has supplanted the traditional professions of their elders. Invariably, these youth regard the official German language as a foreign tongue they have had to learn for purposes of economic survival.

³Hermann Bausinger. *Volkskultur in der technischen Welt* (Stuttgart: Kohlhammer Verlag, 1961) 169. My translation of: "Wer über den Verfall der schönen alten Mundarten klagt, müßte im Grunde auch in die Klage über das Ende des Analphabetentums einstimmen."

⁴Turner 38.

⁵Turner 39.

⁶Turner 41.

⁷Turner borrows the term "liminality" from van Gennep's *Les Rites de Passage.* Van Gennep uses the term to refer to the middle phase in rites of passage, i.e. the ritual stage which marks the separation of the ritual subject from secular order. To some extent, the terms liminality and communitas correspond to Turner's own concept of "antistructure," a state which, in Turner's definition, temporarily frees people from conformity to social structures.

⁸Turner 41.

⁹This is reported by Jochen Schulte-Sasse, "Karl May's Amerika—Exotik und deutsche Wirklichkeit," *Karl May*, ed. Helmut Schmiedt, (Frankfurt: Suhrkamp, 1983) 101-129.

¹⁰For a review and analysis of such Indianist literature—some hostile, some sympathetic to Native Americans—see Roy Harvey Pearce, *The Savages of America: A Study of the Indian and the Idea of Civilization* (Baltimore: Johns Hopkins UP, 1965). For an illuminating recent account see Sherry Sullivan, "A Redder Shade of Pale: The Indianization of Heroes and Heroines in Nineteeth-Century American Fiction," *Journal of the Midwest Modern Language Association*, Spring, 1987, Vol. 20, No. 1, 57-75.

¹¹This estimate is printed in *Meyer's Enzyklopädisches Lexikon*, p. 791.

¹²Fritz Steuben was the pen name of Erhard Wittek, about whom virtually nothing is known. He wrote various Indianist novels in the 1930s and other works into the 1950s and 60s. Some encyclopedias carry a brief entry on him. The newest 14-volume *Der Große Brockhaus* (1980) encyclopedia omits him altogether.

¹³Fritz Steuben, *Der fliegende Pfeil* (Stuttgart: Franckh'sche Verlagshandlung, n. d.) 5.

Stellt euch einmal vor: in das alte Germanien in der Zeit um Christi Geburt mit seinen einfachen Kriegsmitteln, seiner spärlichen Bevölkerung seinen losenBündnissen aus Familien, Sippen, Stämmen wären Leute aus den Jahren 1700 bis 1800 eingerückt, mit allen Waffen der Zivilisation ausgerüstet, mit der ganzen Brutalität und Heuchelei beladen, die den "zivilisierten" Menschen nicht selten "auszeichnet", wenn er Schwächeren, schlechter Bewaffneten gegenübertritt.

Stellt euch ferner vor, daß das Land sechs=, zehn= und zwanzigmal so groß wäre wie Deutschland— und ihr habt ungefähr die Lage, der sich die Indianer in Nordamerika um jene Zeit gegenüber sahen.

Sie sind auch sonst mit den alten Germanen durchaus zu vergleichen: zwar kannten sie in der Hauptsache die Bearbeitung und Verwendung von Metallen noch nicht, aber sie lebten wie die Germanen in befestigten Dörfern von Jagd und Fischfang, kannten schon den Ackerbau, wenn auch nicht in dem Maße wie die Germanen, sie waren Waldvölker, sie waren offenherzig, gastfrei, tapfer und freiheitsliebend, sie übten die Blutrache—sie waren allerdings in Kampfe zügelloser und blutdürstiger als die Germanen—aber sie hatten auch viel mehr Grund dazu. —Zwei hundert Jahre haben die Indianer gegen die eindringende weiße Flut gekämpft. Dort, wo sie einingermaßen gleich an Zahl und Bewaffnung waren, haben sie in den meitsten

Fällen die Weißen aufs Haupt geschlagen—und das Recht war immer auf Seiten der tausendmal betrogenen, verratenen, ausgeplünderten, erbarmungslos von Ort zu Ort gejagten Rothäute. Mut, List, Ausdauer waren auch bei den Weißen zu finden— vor allen Dingen aber hatten die Weißen die Macht.

[14]Turner 41.

[15]Turner 41.

NBC's Docudrama, *Holocaust,* and Concepts of National Socialism in the United States and the Federal Republic of Germany[1]

Bruce A. Murray

In the weeks preceding his visit to Bitburg in the spring of 1985, President Reagan suggested that the time had come to end a chapter in world history (*New York Times,* 22 March 1985). Forty years after the end of World War II, he asserted, the world should shift its focus away from Germany's National Socialist past. It should absolve the Germans of guilt about the past and permit them to concentrate on the challenges of the present, including the fight against Soviet totalitarianism.

Reactions to Reagan's proposal from a wide range of ideological perspectives in the United States, Europe, and elsewhere indicated that many have been unwilling to adopt such changes.[2] The selection committee for the Nobel Peace Prize affirmed the position of those who wish to continue the public debate about National Socialism by awarding the prize in 1986 to Elie Wiesel, one of the most vocal opponents of President Reagan's message at Bitburg. In the Federal Republic of Germany the discussion among historians and cultural critics about the causes for and significance of the Holocaust became a heated debate in the wake of the Bitburg visit.[3] The debate developed around the claims of Ernst Nolte and others that earlier events in world history, most notably the Stalinist purges, had provided a model for and perhaps even motivated the German persecution of the Jews during the Third Reich (*Frankfurter Allgemeine Zeitung,* 6 July 1986). Jürgen Habermas has been the strongest critic of this interpretation, asserting that it is a calculated measure to bolster the Western alliance against the Soviet Union (*Die Zeit,* 7 November 1986). The Federal election of 1987 suggested that many West Germans share his perspective. The Christian Democratic Union (CDU) integrated the Bitburg message into its campaign literature for the election (*Der Spiegel,* 5 January 1987, 101-02) in an effort to increase its share of the electorate beyond 50%. Instead, the CDU percentage decreased, and some analysts cited the Party's campaign ploy as a contributing factor (*Der Spiegel*, 2 February 1987, 6-22).

As the Bitburg event and responses to it demonstrate, what I provisionally will refer to as "American interests" play a significant role in the development of popular images of National Socialism in the Western world. While increasing numbers of Europeans have begun to perceive common interests in opposition to the nuclear arms race, the proponents of a strong Western alliance have attempted to reinforce the old binary distinction between the "evil East" and the "liberating West."[4] From this perspective, the effort to separate contemporary West Germany from its National Socialist past appears as part of a strategy to cast West Germany as a modern ally of the United States and to portray the Soviet Union as an example of, if not the model for, the totalitarianism of the Third Reich.

In this essay I will consider to what extent the Bitburg image of National Socialism reflects the dominant portrayal of that phenomenon in U.S. film and television and to what extent the West German reception of such portrayals foreshadowed its reaction to the Bitburg commemoration. A number of films would provide good examples for the investigation of potential convergences between the narratives of foreign policy and those of cinema and television in the United States.[5] I will concentrate on the production and reception of a single exemplary text, the NBC docudrama *Holocaust* (1978).

I have chosen the *Holocaust* media events because of their suitability for comparative popular cultural analysis. *Holocaust* attracted extremely large television audiences and sparked intense public debates in the United States and the Federal Republic of Germany.[6] The documents generated by those debates provide a wealth of information about the status of each nation's popular culture, their perceptions of one another, and the influence of discourse about the National Socialist past on the development of those perceptions. Comparative analysis of the documents offers valuable insights about the process whereby popular culture provides a forum for and contributes to the changing relationship between two of the strongest allies in the postwar era.

The World War II Combat Narrative as Source of Information about National Socialism in U.S. Cinema and Television

The institutions of film and television in the United States traditionally have portrayed National Socialism almost exclusively within the context of U.S. involvement in World War II.[7] Their narratives about World War II, however, have told us very little about Nazi Germany (Basinger 89-90). Most World War II combat films have constructed a superficial opposition between "evil" Nazis and "brave" Americans. They set difficult goals and suggested that Americans could accomplish them more or less single-handedly. Even in television's *Hogan's Heroes*, it was Captain Hogan's leadership that ensured the success of the prisoners (who represent the Western Allies) in their efforts to dupe their German captors and win the war. By following the strategies of the film industry's classic paradigm,[8] the World War II narratives frequently reflected a cold-war mentality that fostered images of Americans as the morally-justified and capable caretakers of a world threatened by the alleged foes of American democracy.

When doubts about the policies of the United States as the self-proclaimed advocate of world democracy intensified at the end of the 1960s and at the beginning of the 1970s the combat film genre began to disintegrate.[9] During the 1970s, film and television gradually abandoned the World War II combat narrative altogether in favor of more differentiated and critical appraisals of the Korean conflict and the Vietnam War.[10] Films and television series of this type raised questions about the images of the liberating Americans and their tyrannical enemies by dissolving the boundary between opponents and depicting their common, often less than heroic motivations for and responses to war.[11] In the 1980s the traditional combat narrative and its heroes seem to have returned in films and television programs about U.S. conflict with the Soviet Union, Vietnam, and Middle Eastern countries. Noteworthy examples include the *Rambo* series, beginning in 1982, *Red Dawn* (1984), and *Top Gun* (1986).[12]

While the commercial combat narrative almost disappeared and then reappeared, images of National Socialism in cinema and television have experienced little change. During the 1970s and 1980s, occasional films, such as *Hitler, the Last Ten Days* (1973) and television sequels of the *Dirty Dozen* (1987/88), television documentaries, including the British production, *The World at War*, and reruns of *Hogan's Heroes* have provided the primary sources of images in these media. Here, too, most stories have focused very narrowly on the experience of World War II and concentrated on the effects of National Socialism, instead of its causes. Most of them also have perpetuated superficial perceptions of the Americans as liberators and the Germans either as incarnations of evil or as the victims of Hitler's demonic power.[13]

The Production of Holocaust *and its Narrative Project*

As the images of National Socialism associated with the World War II combat film and other movies about World War II moved into the background in the 1970s, the emergence of the television miniseries/docudrama provided the context for the production of the most popular television portrayal of National Socialism—*Holocaust*.[14] In January 1977, while ABC was broadcasting *Roots*, Titus Productions presented Gerald Green's treatment for a docudrama about a Jewish family in Nazi

Germany to NBC. The commercial success of *Roots*, in addition to the quality of Green's treatment, motivated NBC to offer Titus a contract for production immediately. Just fourteen months later *Holocaust: The Story of the Family Weiss* appeared on four consecutive evenings on NBC.[15] Over 120 million people saw all or part of *Holocaust*, making it NBC's most successful broadcast ever (Knilli and Zielinski 76).

The narrative interweaves two primary plotlines: the stories of the Nazi Dorf family and the Jewish Weiss family. It divides the Weiss story into four subplots: one each for the father, mother, and their two sons, Karl and Rudi. The complexity of the Weiss family plotline results in its dominant position within the narrative and legitimizes the subtitle of the docudrama.

The story begins with the Berlin wedding celebration of Karl, the eldest son of the bourgeois, Jewish Weiss family, to Inge Helms, the daughter of petty-bourgeois, Protestant parents. Once the exposition has established tension between the bourgeois, Jewish and petty-bourgeois, non-Jewish characters, the narrative builds around that tension. It interweaves the story of Eric Dorf's rise from poverty as an unemployed lawyer to wealth and prestige as a high-ranking officer in the S.S. with the disintegration of the Weiss family.

In the end only the younger son, Rudi, and Inge Helms survive. Rudi had decided to leave Germany, join the resistance movement, and fight the Nazis with his lover and later wife, Helena. Inge never had ended her struggle to help Karl. She decides to remain in Berlin, and in the final scene Rudi accepts an invitation to supervise a group of orphan boys on their journey to a new home in Palestine.

The manifest historical significance of the subject matter might have influenced the producers of *Holocaust* at least to balance the educational and entertainment components of the docudrama. Their decisions to change the script as it developed from treatment to final screenplay and their published comments indicate that the producers sought no such balance. Instead, they relied heavily on conventional standards of the cinematic and television institutions to maximize commercial success by emphasizing entertainment values (Knilli and Zielinski 79-90). In the process, they reinforced the perception of the ideological opposition that characterizes much of contemporary political discourse.

Very early in the script's development the producers encouraged Gerald Green to change the title from *The Family Weiss* to *Holocaust: The Story of the Family Weiss* (Knilli and Zielinski 48). By changing the title, the producers intensified the suggestion of an historical and emotional spectacle. While encouraging Green to claim that the docudrama would portray the broadest dimensions of Jewish persecution under National Socialism, they also directed him to add the Dorf family plotline (Knilli and Zielinski 48). As a result of such changes, the narrative focused narrowly on the dramatic personal conflict between opposing families, thus diverting attention from economic and political processes that contributed to the rise of National Socialism and the persecution of the Jews.

In addition to personalizing the central conflict, the producers decided to change the expositional sequence, replacing a meeting between Dr. Weiss and Dorf with the mixed marriage celebration of Karl and Inge (Knilli and Zielinski 48). The new expositional sequences establish a more cohesive foundation from which the various plotlines emerge and develop. The exposition allows spectators to identify easily the opposing constellations of characters and provides a fertile setting for more immediate and intense dramatic development. The opening sequences multiply the possibilities for spectators to experience dramatic tension by increasing the number of characters and the amount of interaction between characters. They also encourage spectators to begin the process of emotional engagement, identifying with the members of the congenial Weiss family and sensing discomfort about Hans Helm's appearance in a military uniform as well as his conversations with the Nazi, Heinz Müller.

Thus far my discussion has focused on the producer's desire to maximize commercial success by changing components of the plot. The expositional segment of *Holocaust* also demonstrates its adherence to other commercial standards of narration. Its dependence on continuity editing[16] provides a good example. The opening sequence of *Holocaust* consists almost exclusively of a conventional establishing shot, which sets the spectator's spatial orientation, and shot/reverse-shot series. The pairing of standing toasts by the fathers of the bride and groom, the exchange of glances between the Nazi friend of the bride's family and the uncle of the Jewish groom, as well as the short dialogue between the bride's brother and the groom's grandfather, establish the simple oppositional structure that persists throughout the film. In each case, the continuity of camera angle (mostly eye level), distance (mostly close-up), and movement (minimal pans that never transgress the 180 degree axis) encourage spectators to accept alternating perspectives as plausible. They are well motivated either by the verbal or non-verbal cues of the characters and they maintain the spectator's spatial orientation either as observer within the fictional space or as television spectator.

According to the analysis of Bordwell, et al. (3, 13 and 25-29), the classic narrative is character-centered. Psychological causality motivates its development. It usually confronts the protagonists with an obstacle and portrays their efforts to overcome the obstacle and achieve a goal. And the narrative agent appears to be neutral or, as Christian Metz explains, it functions as an invisible signifier (Metz 91-7). The expositional segment of *Holocaust* has demonstrated the narrative's adherence to the principle of continuity editing. Two additional segments demonstrate clearly its adherence to the other standards of the classic paradigm with the portrayal of the obstacles that confront the Weiss family, as well as their strategies for overcoming them and achieving goals.

In various settings throughout the docudrama Joseph Weiss suggests that love will conquer the persecution that the family confronts. As the narrative progresses and members of the Weiss family perish, the credibility of relying on a love that conquers all diminishes. At the same time, Rudi's strategy of violence becomes more attractive.

The end of the first part of *Holocaust* illustrates the attraction well. At that point Rudi talks to his lover, Helena, about leaving her home in Prague to join him in fighting the National Socialists. He suggests that they have been separated forever from their pasts and now must plan for the future. Helena accepts Rudi's suggestion, and Part I ends with previews of future episodes that succinctly focus the spectator's attention on Rudi's strategy for overcoming obstacles and achieving goals. The preview sequences portray the parallel acceleration of Nazi persecution with the increasing violent opposition of some Jews, suggesting that organized violence is the only effective method to combat fascist behavior.

The Reception of Holocaust in the United States

In religious, educational, and domestic settings, spectators of various age groups and social backgrounds across the nation responded immediately and for weeks following the original broadcast of *Holocaust* in April 1978. The published responses of large percentages of spectators were primarily emotional, focused on *what* happened, instead of *why*, and they were oriented toward ascribing guilt either to the Nazis/Germans or to the Jews.[17] In separate surveys of 411 and 179 randomly chosen spectators from all over the United States (sponsored by the American Jewish Committee [AJC] and Northwestern University, respectively) and in a survey of 2,250 high school students from the Pittsburgh area, many spectators chose characterizations of the docudrama such as "horrifying," "shocking," "moving," and "emotionally involving" (AJC 6, 18; Stern Burstin 24). Large numbers of survey respondents also claimed that *Holocaust* had taught them something. But closer scrutiny reveals that most considered themselves to be better informed only about *what* had happened in National Socialist Germany. In the AJC survey, for example, sixty percent said that the docudrama had helped them to understand better "what Hitler's treatment of the Jews was all about" (AJC 6). When asked whether presenting a program like *Holocaust* was a good idea, eighty-three percent of those who responded positively asserted that it "could make people aware of what might happen" (AJC 9). Each of the cited surveys limited questions about *why* the Holocaust had occurred to questions about collective guilt. Ninety-one percent of those spectators from the AJC survey, who believed that their feelings about the Nazis had been affected, said that the presentation had "strengthened or revealed anti-Nazi feelings" in themselves (AJC 8), Forty-three percent of the Pittsburgh area high school students, who claimed that *Holocaust* had a significant impact on them, asserted that they were left "saddened, sorry, ashamed, angry with the Nazis" (Stern Burstin 24-5). On the other hand, significant numbers of spectators also cited Jewish passivity as a reason for their persecution (AJC 15-16 and Hormuth/Stephan 34). The implicit conclusion for such spectators was that violence was necessary.

As the surveys confirm, *Holocaust* deviated only insignificantly from the conventional portrayal of the National Socialist past in U.S. film and television. Although it featured a Jewish family in a German setting and hinted at the economic and political context during the years immediately preceding World War II, *Holocaust* concentrated only on the effects of National Socialism, personalized history, and affirmed strategies of violence to overcome obstacles and achieve goals. The figure of Rudi, who resembles the stereotypical American youth of the late 1970s in his physical appearance, athletic interests, and temperament, continues the cinematic and television tradition of male individualists whose "independence" paradoxically represents their conformity to the conventional standards for the American hero. Like the heroes of the traditional combat narratives, Rudi spends little time attempting to understand the social dynamics of the problems that confront him. And like contemporary U.S. foreign policy-makers with their characterizations of situations in Europe, the Middle East, and Central America, he quickly identifies the forces of "good" and "evil," strikes out to combat "evil," and apparently succeeds.[18] The portrayal of his success with emotionally engaging, seamless narration encourages spectators to accept Rudi's perception of the world and his strategies for action. As the cited surveys indicate, *Holocaust* did little to stimulate public discussion about the socio-historical and socio-psychological dynamics of fascist behavior. And it did little to promote models for social development that would inhibit the spread of such behavior and render violent opposition superfluous.[19]

Popular Portrayals of National Socialism in the Federal Republic of Germany

A number of factors have contributed to portrayals of National Socialism in the popular culture of West Germany that differ from the dominant American portrayal. The direct experience of National Socialism, the process of formulating an anti-facist national identity within the context of the "Cold War," periodic trials of alleged war criminals, incidents of civil disobedience and the response of state institutions, as well as media events such as the broadcast of *Holocaust* all have nurtured a discussion about fascism that appears to be broader and deeper than similar discussions in the United states. Such discussions have found varied expression in the films of West German cinema and television.

During the first years following World War II, the legacy of National Socialist propaganda (the institutions and its products) significantly influenced the portrayal of images of National Socialism in cinema (Seidl 12-24). The shortage of experienced filmmakers with no connection to National Socialism and the relative ineffectiveness of de-nazification enabled many filmmakers who had made their first films during the Nazi period, or at least found models for production in Nazi cinema, to produce films about the immediate past.[20] The result of this continuity was the renewed dependence on a narrative presence that preached or forcefully persuaded. The only difference was that now films directed spectators to reject National Socialist authority and embrace that of Western-style democracy. In films such as *The Murderers Are Among Us (Die Mörder sind unter uns*, Wolfgang Staudte, 1946) and *Affaire Blum* (Erich Engel, 1948), for example, the narrative discouraged grass-roots initiatives to deal with National Socialists. Instead of encouraging spectators to consider a wide variety of political alternatives to the National Socialist past, these and other films advocated submission to the authority of the existing legal system and to the political parties of bourgeois democracy.[21]

During the "Wirtschaftswunder" of the 1950s, West German filmmakers struggled to compete commercially with Hollywood's cinematic entertainment (Seidl 205-30).[22] In the process, they often portrayed the National Socialist past as nothing more than a backdrop for stories about heroic soldiers who turned against National Socialism but remained loyal to every other aspect of the German heritage (for example, *The Devil's General, Des Teufels General*, Helmut Käutner, 1954). Instead of encouraging spectators to consider the reality of National Socialism and the degree of their responsibility for its atrocities (as did, for example, Bernhard Wicki's *The Bridge, Die Brücke*, 1959), such films allowed spectators to project guilt onto the National Socialist other and identify with the heroic protagonist.

In the 1960s, with the West German film industry's inability to succeed commercially and the emergence of a new generation of filmmakers, things began to change. The representatives of New German Cinema formulated their identities less within the context of National Socialist Germany and its immediate aftermath, and more in opposition to what they perceived as the continuity between the social institutions of the Third Reich and those of West Germany's "Wirtschaftswunder."[23]

They posited the concept of an *Autorenkino* (in which the director replaces the producer as primary authority in the decision-making process), demanded freedom from constraints associated with highly-standardized, commercial film production, and began experimenting with the unconventional narration of *their* stories about contemporary issues.

Very few New German films have portrayed National Socialist Germany, but most of them raise questions about the influence of economic, political, psychological, and perhaps most important, aesthetic theory and practice on the development of fascistic models for social interaction in general. During the 1960s and much of the 1970s, the Third Reich received more direct attention from television than from cinema in West Germany. Filmmakers preferred to investigate other manifestations of fascist behavior. Volker Schlöndorff, for example, portrayed its development in the bourgeois world of *fin de siecle* Austria in *The Young Törless (Der junge Törless*, 1965/66). And R.W. Fassbinder (Fear Eats the Soul, Angst essen Seele auf, 1974) followed its development in contemporary West Germany, where some Germans have prejudged and persecuted the "guest workers."

At the same time, other filmmakers created self-reflexive narratives that encouraged spectators to question the narrative authority of their films and to cooperate in the production of ideology. Alexander Kluge, whose assessment of mass media's dominant methods for the ideological organization of everyday experience provided a model for intellectual critiques of the "culture industry" in the late 1960s and 1970s (Negt/Kluge), also enacted alternative forms of cinematic narration with films such as *Yesterday Girl (Abschied von gestern*, 1965/66) and *The Female Patriot (Die Patriotin*, 1979). In each case, he has attempted to demonstrate that narrative strategies, too, can foster autocratic structures for the production of meaning that resemble those of the National Socialist period, or alternately they can encourage critical and cooperative structures that stimulate the active participation of spectators in the democratic process.[24]

Despite the generation of increasingly differentiated images of fascism/National Socialism in West German popular culture and the efforts of filmmakers and others to foster more active and critical forms of receiving those images, cultural critics often bemoan the relationship of West Germans to their National Socialist past. Some refer to the older generation's reluctance to discuss its past in the public sphere and the younger generation's lack of information about the topic. Critics of this phenomenon posit the concept of collective guilt and repression (Jaspers, and Huyssen 120-1). Others suggest that the broad selection of popular literature on National Socialism and World War II fosters uncritical fascination with the phenomenon (Brüdigam, and Knilli and Zielinski 108). And many assert that discourse about National Socialism figures too prominently in the campaigns of both Germanies and the superpowers to legitimize their social systems. The conservative press in the Federal Republic of Germany frequently characterizes economic explanations for National Socialism as linked too closely to the ideology of the Soviet Union.[25] The leftist press, on the other hand, has criticized emotionally oriented, personalized accounts as products of an industrialized Western culture industry that functions too much like the propaganda industry of the Third Reich (*Ästhetik und Kommunikation, Konkret*, etc.).

The West German Reception of Holocaust

The reception of *Holocaust* in the Federal Republic of Germany exemplified the growing ambivalence toward conventional portrayals of National Socialism in that country[26] The reception was characterized by the tension between the desire to tell one's own story and the desire to allow others to participate in the process of narration, the tension between challenging dominant forms of cinematic representation and the desire to reach a large audience, the tension between the effort to foster critical and collective intellectual activity and the modern spectator's expectation of a private, emotionally-engaging experience.

In the months following the broadcast of *Holocaust* in the United States, news of the event spread throughout West Germany and stimulated widespread criticism (Knilli and Zielinski 107-55). Some critics expressed anger because they considered the U.S. docudrama to be a story which they perceived as a uniquely German story, a story that Germans should tell. Others were offended because of what they perceived as the over-simplifying, commercial entertainment quality of *Holocaust*. Such critics opposed the implication that all non-Jewish Germans had been anti-semitic Nazis and the inadequate attention to the social context within which National Socialism had emerged and gained support. And many critics raised serious questions about the value of broadcasting the docudrama in the Federal Republic of Germany. However, in the fall of 1978 as the 40th anniversary of the *Kristallnacht* approached, and Israel, Great Britain, and Belgium decided to broadcast the series, the leaders of the West Deutscher Rundfunk (West German Broadcast Company) in consultation with other government agencies such as the Federal Center for Political Education (FCPE) decided to set broadcast dates for January 1979 (Zielinski 87).

In an effort to diminish the dominant entertainment quality of the docudrama, while maximizing the potential for public discussion and political education, public institutions initiated a variety of campaigns. Prior to the anniversary of the *Kristallnacht*, the FCPE devised a nation-wide survey on the subject of the Holocaust. Teachers' unions produced teaching aids. The television authorities produced two comprehensive documentaries to prepare the public for the coming film. In the weeks preceding the actual telecast all popular news and television magazines published stories on the Holocaust. Political parties and religious organizations encouraged the public to watch the program. And the broadcasting stations organized live debates with audience participation following each episode.

The docudrama and its subject became the most popular and in some cases almost exclusive topic of public discussion during and for days following the broadcast. In many cities spontaneous public discussions occurred, frequently on the street. Individual calls and letters to the broadcasters reached record levels. And thousands of people who had never talked publicly about their experiences in National Socialist Germany finally began the process of coming to terms in the public sphere.

As was the case in the United States, many of the published audience responses in West Germany fell within the parameters established by the narrative.[27] Large numbers of West German spectators, too, found the docudrama "shocking." Spectators also claimed that the docudrama increased their knowledge of *what* had happened. And many followed the urge to ascribe guilt personally to the Nazis and/or the Jews.

However, in contrast to the United States, where the docudrama's subject evoked more a sense of self-righteousness than guilt among most spectators, for many in West Germany the expression of shock also represented a relatively spontaneous effort to project, deny, or deflect guilt and maintain self-respect.[28] Despite the proliferation of information about the Third Reich during the past four decades, some spectators claimed that they hadn't known about Nazi atrocities, hadn't known the extent of them, or had never considered the personal anguish experienced by the persecuted Jews (Zielinski 133-46 and Ernst 44). Others emphasized that the peoples of other nations had persecuted minorities in the past and that similar behavior persisted into the present in numerous countries, including the United States.[29] A significant minority also agreed with those spectators in the United States who criticized the passivity of the Jews (Hormuth and Stephan 34).

In addition to the implicit desire to lessen or erase a sense of personal responsibility, genuine skepticism about the political effectiveness of commercial film and television products such as *Holocaust* distinguished the published audience responses in the West Germany from those in the United States. The most frequent criticisms cited inadequate attention to historical process and social influences on human behavior. As two respondents from Frankfurt noted:

Mr. Abel: If only they would show what types they are, those who shot the Jews, for example, if they would refuse to do it...

Mr. Brehmer: And how they got to that point, and also, I can't imagine, that somebody goes for the first time, comes there so fresh...and sets himself at a machine gun and starts shooting. And especially also the propaganda, which was made before then, no all that was completely missing.(Prokop 61, my trans.)

The FCPE programs reinforce this sentiment by documenting spectators' needs for further information.[30] Approximately 500,000 people made inquiries following the Center's television announcement that printed guides to the series were available. In response to an FCPE survey question about background information, too, significant percentages expressed the desire to know "why other countries didn't help the Jews" and "why National Socialism found enthusiastic supporters." They also wished to learn more about the "rise of National Socialism and its preconditions" (Ernst 44-5).

Conclusion

As mentioned at the outset, the *Holocaust* media events provide valuable information about the developing relationship of the United States and West Germany to the latter's National Socialist past. They also indicate trends in the developing attitudes of each nation toward the other. And they provide a potential context in which both nations can learn from each other, cooperate in ascribing meaning to the past, and nurture their friendship.

In the United States, *Holocaust* succeeded in part because it reinforced the spectators' most positive images of themselves, their nation, and the nation's function in the world community. Following the experience of Vietnam, Watergate, and the Iran hostage crisis of the 1970s, many Americans had begun to doubt seriously the strength and morality of the United States. In a world that had grown increasingly complex, in which the function of the United States as liberator and protector of world democracy seemed dramatically compromised, the docudrama offered spectators welcome relief. *Holocaust* renewed their trust by presenting an image of a world in which everything falls into easily distinguishable categories of good and evil. Holocaust paid no attention to the inadequate U.S. diplomatic efforts to check the spread of National Socialism nor to the possibility that, for a variety of reasons, some in the United States at least indirectly had supported the Nazis. Instead, it posited a distinctly evil, "German" quality of fascism and implied that the United States, by rejecting pacifism and fighting in World War II, acted (as had Rudi Weiss) with moral justification.[31]

In the Federal Republic of Germany, *Holocaust* seemed to have enabled many spectators to work through lingering feelings of individual/ national guilt and isolation to a sense of shared responsibility and belonging to the world community. By encouraging spectators to identify emotionally with Jewish victims and, from that standpoint, to project guilt onto Germans, with whom they also identified, *Holocaust* made it possible for spectators to accept guilt, but simultaneously to feel separate from the subject of guilt. By emphasizing the ineffectiveness of Jewish pacifism, the docudrama also allowed spectators to project guilt onto the Jews and to perceive shared responsibility.

The programs of the FCPE and other government agencies, too, helped spectators in West Germany integrate their efforts to work through their National Socialist past with efforts to understand better what social processes foster fascistic behavior generally. The process included close scrutiny of the docudrama itself. Within this context, *Holocaust* appeared to many West Germans as part of a much broader tendency in the United States to portray the world as comprised of good and evil and to suggest that good must combat evil with violence. Such portrayals met opposition from increasing numbers of Germans who either associated the National Socialist past with the contemporary situation in West Germany or linked the oppositional structure of *Holocaust* to the heightened tension between the superpowers at the end of the 1970s and beginning of the 1980s.

According to Theodor Adorno, the process of coming to terms with National Socialism will continue until its causes no longer exist (572). In the popular culture of the Federal Republic of Germany the process has included the production of various films. At approximately the same time that *Holocaust* appeared on West German television, Volker Schlöndorff completed *The Tin Drum (Die Blechtrommel,* 1979), an adaptation of Günter Grass's novel about Oskar Matzerath and his experience of fascism in and around Danzig from the turn of the century through the end of World War II. In 1979 other films, including Alexander Kluge's *Female Patriot,* Peter Lilienthal's *David,* and Helma Sanders-Brahms' *Germany, Pale Mother (Deutschland, bleiche Mutter),* too, focused on the National Socialist past and the postwar generation's efforts to come to terms with it.

Typical of these and other films of the 1980s, most notably Edgar Reitz's response to *Holocaust* with the miniseries *Homeland (Heimat,* 1984), is the desire to contextualize National Socialism. In most cases their portrayals focus critically on a process of individual—and national-identity formation predicated on patriarchy, instrumental reason, the power of mass media and a confrontational relationship of self and other.[32] In *Homeland,* for example, Edgar Reitz depicts the transformation of rural Schabbach from a village at the end of World War I into a contemporary city in which men are fascinated with modern technology and employ it in ways that threaten their natural and social environment.[33]

My introductory comments suggested that what I referred to earlier as American interests contribute significantly to reproducing this process of identity formation at every level. However, it may be more accurate to consider the convergence of fictional narratives such as *Holocaust* with political narratives about a nation's past and present as a universal phenomenon. Perhaps the phenomenon merely has manifested itself most clearly in the United States during the past decade. As the contemporary popular culture and political landscapes of Western European countries indicate, what may have originated as an American phenomenon also finds expression elsewhere. Many hallmarks of U.S. culture in the 1980s, including everything from neo-conservatism, to tax reform and *Dallas* find a sizable constituency in Western European countries, too.[34]

At the same time, the West German reception of *Holocaust* and a variety of other events, including everything from the NATO allies' response to the summit in Reykjavik to the 1987 visit by Erich Honecker to Bonn, suggest resistance to the influence of the dominant U.S. (and Soviet) culture. The West European ambivalence toward what Michael Rogin calls "political demonology" seems to be intensifying. And that ambivalence is by no means limited to Western Europe. Efforts to recast the relationship between individuals. groups, and nations as non-oppositional and cooperative are under way in everything from feminist film criticism (Mayne 19) to U.S./Soviet relations. Even President Reagan contributed to the change during the 1987 Washington summit. By invoking the popular culture of the Soviet Union, referring to the nuclear arms race as the bear who does not permit the soldier who has captured it to present it to his commanding officer, he once again mixed fiction and reality, but in a way that may have provided a foundation for new thinking about the relationship between individuals and between nations.

Notes

[1]This essay is the revised and expanded version of a paper that I presented at the 1987 MLA convention.

[2]For selected examples, see Geoffrey Hartman, ed., *Bitburg in Moral Perspective* (Bloomington: Indiana UP, 1986) 173-233.

[3]For a good selection of contributions to the debate, see *"Historikerstreit"* (Munich: Piper, 1987).

[4]For a more detailed account of this phenomenon, see Robert Dallek, *Ronald Reagan, The Politics of Symbolism* (Cambridge: Harvard UP, 1984) 129-62.

[5]Michael Rogin has demonstrated most convincingly that there is a convergence between contemporary foreign policy and the dominant narrative models of cinema and television. See his *Ronald Reagan, the Movie* (Berkeley: U of California P, 1987) 1-43.

[6]The best source of information about the production and reception of *Holocaust* is *Holocaust zur Unterhaltung*, eds. Friedrich Knilli and Siegfried Zielinski, West Berlin: Elefanten, 1982.

[7]Popular feature films about World War II have included *The Longest Day* (1962), *The Battle of the Bulge* (1966), *The Dirty Dozen* (1967), *Patton* (1969), and *Kelly's Heroes* (1970). The most popular television series have included *Combat, Twelve O'Clock High*, and, of course, *Hogan's Heroes*. For more detailed information about

the portrayal of National Socialism in U.S. cinema and television, see Jeanine Basinger, *The World War II Combat Film. Anatomy of a Genre* (New York: Columbia UP, 1986); Bernhard F. Dick, *The Star-Spangled Screen* (Lexington: UP of Kentucky, 1985); Annette Insdorf, *Indelible Shadows* (New York: Random House, 1983).

[8]For a detailed description of the paradigm and its development, see David Bordwell, et al. *The Classical Hollywood Cinema* (New York: Columbia UP, 1985). I will discuss the quality and significance of the paradigm below in my analysis of the *Holocaust* narrative.

[9]The disintegration manifested itself initially in the transformation of the impeccable World War II combat hero into a flawed, although still sympathetic protagonist. For a more detailed discussion, see Basinger: 201-19.

[10]Isolated films, such as *The Green Berets* (1968), followed the combat model in plot development and in narrative style, but more typical of the new trend were *M.A.S.H.* (1970), *Apocalypse Now* (1977), and the television series *M.A.S.H.*

[11]While reflecting the public's intensifying confusion about the role of the United States and its military in plot development and characterization, such portrayals also experimented with less conventional narrative techniques that drew attention to the increasing ambivalence. The consistent voice-over narration in *Apocalypse Now* and the spoken letters from the front in television's *M.A.S.H.* created the format for soldiers to express uncertainty about the meaning of portrayed experiences. (This technique also was adopted for *Platoon* [1987], one of the most popular "combat" films of the 1980s.) By focusing on characters who struggled within the narrative framework to understand and evaluate their experiences, instead of relying on conventional omniscient story-tellers, such films challenged spectators to perceive the limitations of narrative perspective, contemplate other perspectives, and in the process, participate more actively in ascribing meaning to cinematic and television portrayals of a reality that had become far less transparent.

[12]Although it seems very plausible that the changing political climate in the United States has contributed to the apparent demise and recuperation of the conventional combat film over the past three decades, it is also likely that the desire to vary the genre marginally, a typical strategy of standardized commercial film production, has provided at least the possibility for changes in plot structure and characterization.

[13]Some films, such as *The Battle of Britain* (1969) and *A Bridge Too Far* (1977, technically a British production) have portrayed individual Germans as critics of the Nazi regime, but in most cases such portrayals accentuate the critical individual's helplessness and function primarily to emphasize the necessity of allied intervention. Even less frequent have been films, such as *Ship of Fools* (1965), which offer a more differentiated image of German society and stimulate critical reflection about the susceptibility of some Germans to the Nazi ideology.

[14]At the beginning of the decade the Public Broadcasting System experienced considerable success with its short-term British series. The major networks monitored the success and began to experiment with their own miniseries/docudramas. After NBC had attracted phenomenal television audiences with *Rich Man, Poor Man* (1976) and *Roots* (1977), the other networks accelerated their efforts to compete for the miniseries audience. In what follows I will refer to those multi-episode productions that claim an association with a specific event in world history as docudramas. I will refer to multi-episode productions in general as miniseries.

[15]For more detailed information about the production and reception of *Holocaust*, see, among others, Friedrich Knilli, and Siegfried Zielinski, eds. *Holocaust zur Unterhaltung*. West Berlin: Elefanten, 1982; and Yitzhak Ahren, et al. *Das Lehrstück 'Holocaust'*. (Opladen: Westdeutscher, 1982).

[16]Continuity editing is the use of shot-reverse shot sequences, match cuts, and other editing techniques to create the impression of a smooth, seamless progression of images and erase the source of enunciation.

[17]It is worth noting that professional analysts monitored a variety of audience responses and in many cases affirmed the response parameters that had been established by the narrative. They focused attention on the docudrama's emotional appeal by providing response selections that referred almost exclusively to that component. And they reinforced the perception that National Socialism was primarily a personalized conflict between members of opposing ethnic groups by asking spectators to decide to which characters guilt should be ascribed.

[18]It is important to note here that, while the dominant narrative style of contemporary foreign policy does seem to converge with that of cinematic and television entertainment, the corresponding messages about the Germans diverge. In foreign policy, as in cinema and television, the narrative style affirms the existence of absolutely distinct nationalities and ideologies, privileges that of the United States, and discourages critical reflection about potential common needs and strategies for fulfilling those needs. However, while U.S. foreign policy has developed an image of the Federal Republic of Germany as a close ally that deserves our protection, cinema and television generally have limited their portrayals to those that depict Germans as our National Socialist enemies. In other words, while cinema and television have functioned to solidify the perception of the United States as liberator in the struggle against the Nazis, U.S. foreign policy replaces the Germans with the Soviets and sustains the image of liberating Americans.

[19]In "The Politics of Identification," *New German Critique* 19 (1980): 117-36, Andreas Huyssen questions critics who valorize a reception aesthetic based on rational discourse. He associates such critics and their thinking with the failed student movement of the 1970s in West Germany and challenges them to embrace emotionally-engaging narration as manifested in *Holocaust*. His argument is that *Holocaust* enabled many Germans for the first time to identify with Jewish victims of Nazi persecution and to establish the distance from their own past necessary to formulate a critique. But what is the value of this critique? One also could argue that the narrative strategy of the *Holocaust* docudrama only perpetuated the projection of guilt that, according to the Mitscherlichs, has characterized the German response to National Socialism since 1945. *Holocaust* may have encouraged spectators to perceive German responsibility that lies in the past and is distinct from those of contemporary Germans who must decide whether or not something similar could happen again. In addition, it is possible that the nation-wide programs to stimulate public debate about *Holocaust* in West Germany before and after the broadcast contributed significantly to the intensity of reception that Huyssen affirms in his essay. I will return to this point below.

[20]Examples, including Helmut Käutner's *In Those Days (In jenen Tagen*, 1947) and Erich Engel's *Affaire Blum* (1948), employed for the most part the emotionally-engaging, seamless narration that German cinema had developed in competition with Hollywood cinema during the 1920s. The same techniques also served the National Socialists in their campaigns to influence public opinion and entertain between 1933 and 1945.

[21]For more detailed accounts of postwar German cinema and its portrayal of the immediate past, see, among others, Peter Pleyer, *Deutscher Nachkriegsfilm 1946-48* (Münster: Fahle 1965); Klaus Kreimeier, *Kino und Filmindustrie in der BRD* (Kronberg: Scriptor, 1973); and Siegfried Zielinski, "Faschismusbewältigung im frühen deutschen Nachkriegsfilm," *Sammlung 2. Jahrbuch für antifaschistische Literatur und Kunst*, ed. Uwe Naumann (Frankfurt a.M., 1979) 124-33.

²²At the same time, the filmmakers of the young German Democratic Republic produced conventional narratives that associated anti-fascist resistance with the dominant political forces of East German society (see, for example, Kurt Maetzig's two-part *Ernst Thälmann* epic, 1954-55).

²³For more detailed accounts of New German Cinema, see, among others, Joe Hembus, *Der deutsche Film kann gar nicht besser Sein. Ein Pamphlet von gestern. Eine Abrechnung von heute* (Munich: Rogner & Bernhard, 1981); Alexander Kluge, *Bestandsaufnahme: Utopie Film* (Frankfurt a.M.: Zweitausendeins, 1983; John Sandford, *New German Cinema* (London: Oswald Wolf, 1980); Hans Günther Pflaum and Hans Helmut Prinzler, *Cinema in the Federal Republic of Germany*, trans. Timothy Nevill (Bonn: Inter Nationes, 1983); and Eric Rentschler, *West German Film in the Course of Time* (New York: Redgrave, 1984).

²⁴For more information on Kluge's aesthetics, see, among others, Miriam Hansen, "Space of history, language of time," in: *German Film and Literature. Adaptations and Transformations*, ed. Eric Rentschler (New York: Methuen, 1986) 193-216. Kluge has argued convincingly that institutionalized forms of modern mass media, including film, function less as objective sources of information about everyday life for citizens who wish to take part in the democratic process and more as the subjective organizers of information. As a result, they often function more to limit possible evaluations of everyday experience rather than encouraging the critical and cooperative reception of media events. See his "Die Macht der Bewußtseinsindustrie und das Schicksal unserer Öffentlichkeit," in:*Industrialisierung des Bewußtseins*, eds, Klaus von Bismarck et al. (Munich: Piper, 1985) 51-129, for Kluge's most recent assessment of this phenomenon.

²⁵For more detailed information about the most powerful conservative media conglomerate in West Germany, see Günter Walraff's *Der Aufmacher* (Köln: Kiepenheuer und Witsch, 1982).

²⁶For more detailed accounts of the reception of *Holocaust* in the Federal Republic of Germany, see, among others, issues of *Medium* 9 (1979); *New German Critique* 19 (1980); and the *International Journal of Political Education* 4:1,2 (1981). See also Friedrich Knilli and Siegfried Zielinski eds., *Holocaust zur Unterhaltung* (West Berlin: Elefanten, 1982); and Yitzhak Ahren, et al., *Das Lehrstück 'Holocaust'* (Opladen: Westdeutscher, 1982). For information about the reception in the German Democratic Republic, see H. Kleinschmid, 'Ein Weg ohne Ende.' Zur Reaktion der DDR auf 'Holocaust,' in *Deutschland-Archiv* 12:3 (1979) 225-28.

²⁷My comments here are based on surveys conducted by the Federal Center for Political Education (random sample of 1,000 viewers and 800 non-viewers), Stefan Hormuth and Walter Stephan (random sample of 145 viewers), and Dieter Prokop (23 interviews with 50 residents of Frankfurt). Reports on each of these appeared in the aforementioned issue of the *International Journal of Political Education*. I also have referred to data collected by Friedrich Knilli and Siegfried Zielinski from various discussion evenings during the telecast of the docudrama as reported in their *"Holocaust" zur Unterhaltung* 108-155.

²⁸The survey conducted by Hormuth and Stephan documents this process most graphically. According to their argument, the extremely emotional content of the docudrama stimulates "strong defense mechanisms, such as denial, rationalization, a need to attribute responsibility..."(30).

²⁹It should be noted here that the desire to identify and overcome persecution in all societies only partially motivated comments about similarities between the United States and Germany. An equally strong motivation for spectators, who perceived *Holocaust* as a product of American culture that unjustly condemned the German people, was the desire to defend themselves by deflecting the perceived criticism so that others, including Americans, would be forced to share it.

[30]Once again, it is important to note that, as was the case in the United States, surveys in the Federal Republic of Germany influenced audiences' responses. There was no guarantee that spectators spontaneously would request background information. However, the West German survey anticipated the need for such information and provided spectators with a selection of possible categories. It is at any rate significant that large numbers of respondents *did* select formulations that indicated their desire to identify possible causes for National Socialism.

[31]From the contemporary standpoint, it is also interesting to note that, in the process, *Holocaust* also affirmed the uncritical alliance between the United States and those victims of National Socialism in Israel who have perceived as unavoidable the violent defense of their national interests.

[32]It is evident that critical theory figures prominently in the work of many West German filmmakers. For an introduction to critical theory and its assessment of the modern "culture industry," see David Held's *Introduction to Critical Theory* (Berkeley: U of California P, 1980).

[33]For more information about the production of *Heimat* and its quality as a response to *Holocaust*, see Edgar Reitz, *Liebe zum Kino* (Köln: KOLN 78, 1984) esp. 98-105 and 134-215. See also the *New German Critique* 36 (1985) special issue on *Hiemat*.

[34]The changing cultural landscape of West Germany provides an excellent example. Two years after the Republican, Ronald Reagan, moved into the White House, the Christian Democrat, Helmut Kohl, became *Bundeskanzler*. Shortly after the U.S. Congress passed tax reform legislation in 1986, the *Bundestag* passed similar legislation. During the same period, West German television experienced great success with U.S. television programs, including *Dallas, Dynasty,* etc.

Works Cited

Adorno, Theodor. "Was bedeutet Aufklärung?" In: *Gesammelte Schriften*. Ed. Rolf Tiedemann. 19 vols. Frankfurt a.M.: Suhrkamp, 1977. 10.2: 555-72.

Ahren, Yitzhak, et al. *Das Lehrstück 'Holocaust'*. Opladen: Westdeutscher, 1982.

American Jewish Committee. "Americans Confront the Holocaust." *International Journal of Political Education* 4:1,2 (1981): 5-19.

Asthethik and Kommunikation.

Basinger, Jeanine. *The World War II Combat Films: Anatomy of a Genre*. New York: Columbia UP, 1986.

Bordwell, David, et al. *The Classical Hollywood Cinema*. New York: Columbia UP, 1985.

Brüdigam, Hans. *Der SchoB ist fruchtbar noch...* Frankfurt a.M.: Röderberg, 1965.

Burstin, Barbara Stern. "The 'Holocaust' Reverberates in Pittsburgh." *International Journal of Political Education* 4:1,2 (1981): 21-27.

Dick, Bernhard F. *The Star-Spangled Screen*. Lexington: UP of Kentucky, 1985.

Dallek, Robert. *Ronald Reagan. The Politics of Symbolism*. Cambridge: Harvard UP, 1984.

Der Spiegel 5 January and 2 February 1987.

Ernst, Tilman. " 'Holocaust': Incentives-Reactions-Consequences. The Television Event From the Viewpoint of Political Education." Trans. Gloria Custance. *International Journal of Political Education* 4:1,2 (1981): 37-56.

Frankfurter Allgemeine Zeitung. 6 July 1986.

Habermas, Jürgen. "Vom öffentlichen Gebrauch der Historie." *Die Zeit* 7 November 1986: 4.

Hansen, Miriam. "Space of history, language of time. In: *German Film and Literature. Adaptations and Transformations.* Ed. Eric Rentschler. New York: Methuen, 1986: 193-216.

Hartman, Geoffrey, ed. *Bitburg in Moral and Political Perspective.* Bloomington: Indiana UP, 1986.

Held, David. *Introduction to Critical Theory.* Berkeley: U of California P, 1980.

Hembus, Joe. *Der Deutsche Film kann gar nicht besser sein. Ein Pamphlet von gestern. Eine Abrechnung von heute.* Munich: Rogner & Bernard, 1981.

Hormuth, Stefan and Walter Stephan. "Blaming the Victim: Effects of Viewing 'Holocaust' in the United States and Germany." *International Journal of Political Education* 4:1,2 (1981): 29-35.

Huyssen, Andreas. "The Politics of Identification." *New German Critique* 19 (1980): 117-36.

Insdorf, Annette. *Indelible Shadows.* New York: Random House, 1983.

International Journal of Political Education 4:1,2 (1981).

Jaspers, Karl. *Die Schuldfrage.* Munich: Piper, 1979.

Kleinschmid, H. "'Ein Weg ohne Ende.' Zur Reaktion der DDR auf 'Holocaust.' *Deutschland-Archiv* 12:3 (1979) 225-28.

Kluge, Alexander, ed *Bestandsaufnahme: Utopie Film.* Frankfurt a.M.: Zweitausendeins, 1983.

―――. "Die Macht der BewuBtseinsindustrie und das Schicksal unserer ö´ffentlichkeit,: in *Industrialisierung des BewuBtseins,* eds. Klaus von Bismarck et al. (Munich: Piper, 1985) 51-129.

Knilli, Friedrich and Siegfried Zielinski, eds. *Holocaust zur Unterhaltung.* West Berlin: Elefanten, 1982.

Konkret.

Kreimeir, Klaus. *Kino und Filmindustrie in der BRD.* Kronberg: Scriptor, 1973.

Kühnl, Reinhard. "Die Auseinandersetzung mit dem Faschismus in der BRD und DDR." In: *BRD-DDR. Ein Vergleich der Gesellschaftssysteme.* Ed. Jung, H. et al. Köln: Pahl-Rugenstein, 1971: 248-78.

Mayne, Judith. "Feminist Film Theory and Women at the Movies." *Profession 87.* New York: MLA, 1987: 14-19.

Medium 9 (1979).

Metz, Christian. *The Imaginary Signifier.* Trans. Celia Britton, et al. Bloomington: Indiana UP, 1982.

Mitscherlich, Alexander and Margarete. *The Inability to Mourn.* Trans. Beverley Placfek. New York: Grove, 1975.

Negt, Oskar and Alxander Kluge. *Öffentlichkeit und Erfahrung. Zur Organisation von bürgerlicher und proletarischer Öffentlichkeit.* Frankfurt a.M.: Suhrkamp, 1972.

New German Critique 19 (1980) and 36 (1985).

New York Times 22 March 1985.

Pflaum, Hans Günther and Hans Helmut Prinzler. *Cinema in the Federal Republic of Germany.* Trans. Timothy Nevill. Bonn: Inter Nationes, 1983.

Pleyer, Peter. *Deutscher Nachkriegsfilm 1946-48.* Münster: Fahle, 1965.

Prokop, Dieter. "'Holocaust' and the Effects of Violence on Television." *International Journal of Political Education* 4:1,2 (1981): 57-74.

Reitz, Edgar. *Liebe zum Kino.* Köln: KØLN 78, 1984.

Rentschler, Eric. *West German Film in the Course of Time*. New York: Redgrave, 1984.

Rogin, Michael. *Ronald Reagan, the Movie and Other Episodes in Political Demonology*. Berkeley: U of California P, 1987.

Rosenfeld, Alvin. *Imagining Hitler*. Bloomington: Indiana UP, 1985.

Sanford, John. *New German Cinema*. London: Oswald Wolf, 1980.

Seidl, Claudius. *Der Deutsche Film der fünfziger Jahre*. Munich: Heyne, 1987.

Wallraff, Günter. *Der Aufmacher*. Köln: Kiepenheuer und Witsch, 1982.

Zielinski, Siegfried. "Faschismusbewältigung im frühen deutschen Nachkriegsfilm." *Sammlung 2. Jahrbuch für antifaschistische Literatur und Kunst*. Ed. Uwe Naumann. Frankfurt a.M., 1979: 124-33.

Singing Against Hunger:
French and American
Popular Musicians' Efforts at Charity

André J.M. Prévos

Cultural relations between France and the United States are usually approached at the level of so-called "elite" culture, while popular culture relations and their effects are often noticed (and usually decried) but seldom studied. The rejection of American influences in France has been widely illustrated—for example by the creation of successive Governmental Commissions on Language, whose role was to rid French vocabulary of Anglo-Saxon expressions, with varied and often temporary success. Nevertheless, the adoption of American popular culture elements to French life has not slowed, from the use of CB radio the popularity of Afro-American music, among other elements (Prévos (a), Prévos (b)).

The phenomenon of French and American contributions to the international relief effort on behalf of Ethiopia between 1984 and 1986 provides a rare opportunity for a comparative study since both efforts were inspired by a British initiative. By focusing on the history of each project, the contents of the songs recorded for the occasion and the reactions to each of the undertakings in its country of origin, it becomes possible to compare and contrast the systems of thought that underlie American and French society. On the one hand, it can be argued that some American influence took place (the American song became popular in France); on the other hand such influence was neither unexpected nor exceptional. This essay in comparative popular culture will juxtapose two sets of data for the purpose of underlining cultural differences that owe at least as much to the *mentalité* or national character of each nation as to the situation that led to the production of said data.

Backgrounds

Recent years have witnessed the unexpected development of a movement within the world's popular music establishment. The use of the public support enjoyed by the stars of popular music to help alleviate human tragedy. These "mega-charity" efforts (O'Connor 25) focused at first upon the plight of malnourished populations in the Sahelian areas of Africa and particularly upon the desperate situation in Ethiopia. Once the pattern was established, many other groups were targeted for help and money was raised at special concerts or through the sale of specially recorded songs. This was not an unprecedented tactic. The 1971 Bangladesh Concert and the MUSE "no nukes" concerts of 1978 come to mind. But 1984-1986 was marked by significant new developments both at the organizational and artistic levels.

This essay will deal primarily with American and French efforts to aid the hungry of Ethiopia: the "We Are The World/USA for Africa" project in the United States and the *"Ethiopie/Chanteurs Sans Frontières"* project in France. On both sides of the Atlantic there were other projects involving popular music stars that raised money for other deserving causes: for example, the "Sun City" album against the racial policy in South Africa by Artists United Against Apartheid gathered around Little Steven Van Zandt (Schuers 17, Barol (a) 94) and the "Farm Aid"[1] concerts, deriving primarily from efforts by Willie Nelson and John Cougar Mellencamp to publicize the hardships of American farmers (Gates 24-28, Zimmerman 1D, Hellmich & *al.* 1D). Less musically oriented undertakings included fund-raising efforts such as "Sport Aid" co-sponsored by "Band Aid" and UNICEF ("Geldof's Newest Game" 2D "Famine..."28), as well as the "Hands Across America" celebration to help the hungry ("Bringing the Hunger Fight Home"). On the French side, besides "Chanteurs Sans Frontières" (to be considered later), there was the early "Opération Sahel 84" (Potel 470-473), the "Tam Tam pour l'Ethiopie" record project, whose bluntly-worded promotional ads— "Ethiopia is dying. You owe it 46 francs" (the price of the record)[2]— underlined the urgency of the situation ("Reflet des ventes"), and the concert against racism of 15-16 June, 1985, in Paris, which counted "Chanteurs Sans Frontières" among the cast of performers ("Manifestation anti-raciste" 2). By 1986, charitable operations of this type had spread all over the world, reaching even the Soviet Union, where the "Tchernobyl Aid" concert took place on 31 May (Cooper & Strasser 36).

As the above list suggests, this general form of fund-raising has now achieved world-wide acceptance.[3] However, it is safe to say that the whole movement for African famine relief originated in Great Britain as the brainchild of Bob Geldof, lead singer of Boomtown Rats who, late in 1984, set up the "Band Aid" session. This gathering of popular artists and performers recorded "Do They Know It's Christmas?", a seven-inch single album whose sales quickly skyrocketed on both sides of the Atlantic. The record and its accompanying videocassette were certified gold on 19 December, 1984, after the Recording Industry Association of America waved a rule requiring a sixty-day delay between release and certification; by then, the song had leaped from number 65 to number 20 on *Billboard's* Hot 100 (Grein (b) 3). It soon became evident that the "hundreds of thousands of dollars" of benefit anticipated by the experts would grow into millions; the sum of $3.5 million for Britain alone was quoted soon afterwards ("Special Report: UK...")[4] As the "Brand Aid" contributions poured into the Ethiopian famine relief fund in Great Britain, a few American stars decided to launch their project, while in France other popular performers were thinking about their own effort in favor of Ethiopia.

The American and French Projects: Their Histories

After several weeks of rumors about the names of potential participating artists and efforts aimed at a strict enforcement of licensing agreements on the part of the organizers (Grein 1, Goodman 22) "USA For Africa" was launched. It had been sparked by Harry Belafonte who heard about the African famine and the "Band Aid" effort and became upset by the lack of incentives on the part of black American artists. Belafonte knew Ken Kragen, who had been the manager of the late Harry Chapin, one of the few artists to promote the fight against world famine until his death in 1981. Belafonte wanted to help arrange for a fund-raising concert, but Kragen suggested instead an effort in the style of "Band Aid," adding that black as well as the white popular artists should participate (Breslin, *passim*)[5]

At the time, Kragen was the manager of both Kenny Rogers and Lionel Richie; he contacted the latter about Belafonte's suggestion. Richie immediately committed to writing the song and contacted Stevie Wonder, who agreed to help. Kragen asked Quincy Jones to produce the recording and Jones convinced Michael Jackson to pitch in on the song. Once the production and songwriting details had been solved, Kragen still had to take care of the practical and financial aspects of the enterprise: time and studio, a not-for-profit corporation to channel the funds, and financial resources to pay for expenses not covered by donated services (Rogers and Richie would donate $200,000). Kragen also had to organize the gathering together of artists in Los Angeles on a given date and at a given place (Breslin *passim*).

Owing to previous commitments, Wonder could not actively participate in the writing of the song; Richie and Jackson would have to do it themselves, with gentle but constant prodding by Quincy Jones. By 16 January, 1985, Jackson had finished composing the music and, a week later, after a few meetings between the composers, the lyrics were added: the song "We Are the World" was ready to be recorded. Its composers had wanted it to be something grand in tempo, a sort of anthem in the vein of "Let it Be" and "Bridge Over Troubled Water."

The song was recorded on 28 January, 1985, at the A & M studios in Los Angeles. The date had been chosen because most of the forty-six artists who had agreed to participate and lend their names to this effort were already in Los Angeles for the American Music Awards ceremony scheduled for that evening. It was then decided that the artists would come directly to the studio after the Awards ceremony and that the recording would take place overnight. The recording session was also video-taped for presentation by cable-television networks and for future sale to the public (Grein (c) 1).

The artists' efforts received enthusiastic support from their respective recording and publishing companies, whose advertisements soon filled the pages of the trade and specialized journals and magazines. This public effusion on the part of the conglomerates was also often backed by financial contributions, the most common being allowing the artists to record for the company (CBS) that issued the record and to donate the profits to the "USA For Africa" foundation. By the end of March, 1985, prospects for the sale of the "We Are The World" record—to be issued 7 April—looked very promising: the anticipated revenue from the sale of video cassettes and television broadcasts—by HBO and MTV—as well as from the sale of video cassettes of the recording session and from assorted merchandise (T-shirts, pins, buttons, etc.) generated euphoria among the founders and members of the "USA For Africa" foundation (Ware 4).

By early April the trade publications featured articles about the record and many of them published special issues commemorating the event. The record debuted on *Billboard's* Top Pop Album Chart at number nine ("Dealers Cheer 'World' Album" 1.) By the end of April, the single was at the top of the charts in Great Britain, West Germany, The Netherlands, and Australia; it was number two in Japan, and number six in Canada (behind the Canadian recording for Ethiopia). This rapid rise to the top of the international charts was followed by an equally swift fall: the single did not spend more than six weeks at the top of the charts—only the album lasted somewhat longer in the ratings—due to what analysts described as a "relatively fast burnout rate" (Grein (a) 6).

The origins of the Ethiopian aid in France were quite different, but not totally unrelated to those of "USA for Africa." In France, in and around Paris, during the month of December, 1984, concerts were organized by French popular entertainer Daniel Guichard to benefit the humanitarian association headed by Abbé Pierre, a French Catholic priest known for his efforts in behalf of the poor, the hungry, the homeless, and the abandoned (Rioux 74). Early in January, 1985, French artist Valérie Lagrange heard the "Band Aid" recording while in Great Britain. She alerted Renaud, one of the most popular stars of French popular music, who then decided to organize other French artists in order to duplicate Geldof's efforts. During the few weeks it took Renaud and his associate Coluche, France's foremost comic at that time, to organize their project both the "USA for Africa" and the "Tam Tam Pour l'Ethiopie" recordings had been published. The popular success of these two records convinced Renaud and Coluche to press forward and issue their own record as fast as they possibly could.

The song "Ethiopie" was written by Renaud with collaboration from Frank Langloff. As had been the case with the American recording, studio time was donated and the composer donated his royalties to the cause. The respective recording and publishing companies of each of the participants agreed to the presence of their artists on a record produced by another company and deeded all the benefits to the association "Médecins Sans Frontières," a group of physicians known for their interventions all over the world on behalf of victims of natural and human disasters. At that time, "Médecins Sans Frontières" had some of its members already in the Sahel as well as in Afghanistan. Since there already existed an organization capable of receiving and channeling funds to relieve hunger in Africa, the French artists decided to donate all revenues to "Médecins Sans Frontières" without establishing a not-for-profit organization to disseminate funds raised. By calling themselves "Chanteurs Sans Frontières" the French artists also reinforced their clear connection with the "Medecins Sans Frontières" organization.

During the month of April, 1985, Renaud and Coluche assembled thirty-four other French popular artists (a few of them not pop singers) and entertainers. They recorded the song "Ethiopie" and issued it on a twelve-inch single (the back side being an instrumental version of the song). For a French production aimed primarily at a French-speaking or simply French audience the record was successful, selling more than one million copies by 31 May, 1985. On 2 June, 1985, Coluche was thus able to present a check in the amount 10,000,000 French Francs (about $1,500,000) to Ronny Brauman, President of "*Médecins Sans Frontières*" ("Quand Coluche dribble. . ." 44).

As is now evident, the actual production of the recordings and the distribution of each of the songs recorded in France and in America followed similar patterns. Both groups of artists used Geldof's initiative and created their own projects. To be sure, the American project was on a somewhat grander scale, more artists were involved and, more importantly, owing to the geographical distribution of the latter, there was a need for more coordination. The American Music Awards ceremony provided a welcome answer to Kragen and his associates. In France, the geographical problems were non-existent because France is, after all, a small country and most of the popular artists live in Paris. In addition, the majority of French recording studios are located in and around the city. As a consequence, the French project was much easier to put together and organize. Where the American organizers spent more than four months between the writing of the song and the sale of the first record, the French spent less than two months.

The major organizational difference between the projects had to do with the fact that the French artists already knew what to do with the anticipated revenue of the "Chanteurs Sans Frontières" operation. The American artists had no such ready-made solution, hence the need for the creation of the "USA For Africa" foundation. The name of the American foundation, "USA For Africa," suggests both a national and continental involvement; the name "Chanteurs Sans Frontières" suggests more of an outgrowth of an already existing movement. But these differences, primarily due to the situations encountered by the organizers of each of the projects, cannot hide the fact that these were launched after Geldof's original efforts and were purposefully patterned after his own project.

"We Are The World" and "Ethiopie": Two Songs, Two Records

The publication of the "We Are The World" record in America did not lead to any uneasiness among the artists who were not featured on the record sleeve. There is no evidence to suggest that these artists suffered from any backlash or from a marked disaffection on the part of the American public. The publication of the "Ethiopie" record in France, however, caused a short-lived politically-inspired protest from several popular artists who had not been asked to participate in the recording of the song.[6] This brief episode ("Ram Dam pour l'Ethiopie" 24) was quickly forgotten.

A reading of the lyrics of each of the songs reveals differences in the respective approaches used by Richie and Jackson on the one hand and by Renaud and Langloff on the other. (The lyrics of both songs are included in the Appendix; a transliteration—not a literary translation—of the French song is also included). "We Are The World" focuses more on a general problem—that of a people dying—and on the need for the world to come together to help, to "heed a certain call", than it does on the special plight of famine-stricken Ethiopia. The gift expected from everyone would be a gift of life—the family of God united by love, as is suggested by the Beatles—inspired line, "Love is all we need." The chorus reinforces this image, all the while exhorting—"Let's start giving"—to help bring about "a better day." The chorus also insists upon the relevancy of the effort: we are not only helping save someone else's life but "we're saving our own lives....Just you and me." It is only in the third stanza and through the use of a biblical metaphor that hunger appears in the song. The rousing call of the last verse, later repeated as a bridge by several artists taking solos each in their turn, as well as the powerful message of its last line—"When we stand together as one"—reinforce the dire need for solidarity if we and our world are to survive.

The idea of solidarity, at least among the performers, was reinforced in two ways. First, the solos taken by some of the singers were not identified on the records but only in some of the lyrics. Second, the record sleeve featured the drop picture of all the artists in front of a "USA For Africa" banner; they were not to be seen as a gathering of individual stars, but as a group of participants in a communal effort (it was said that "egos had to be checked at the studio door.")

The French song "Ethiopie," even though similar in emphasis, nevertheless differs in content from "We Are The World." The need for solidarity is clear: "Let us give them life/Only life;" but the abject situation is also vividly suggested. Ethiopia is pictured as an "Abandoned sailship without sails or oars," awaiting a wind to escape the doldrums. The song itself is described as a small effort on the performers' part, but if "we could just do this song" and give, there would be another chance for those dying from thirst and hunger. The children are dying "away from our hearts," out of sight out of mind: we must open our eyes to a country's lingering death. These deaths threaten all of us: the death of each child "darkens the sky" a little more and reduces our future. The need to insure the survival of Ethiopia and its people is illustrated through a brutal image based on well-documented facts: acid rain, so infamous in Western Europe, causes "the forest to pass away." Meanwhile, in Sahelian Africa and in Ethiopia in particular "the desert advances faster than the dove." Desertification is a peril faced by all of mankind. What requires our efforts is to "silence silence itself" putting an end to the "sky of indifference," below which such tragic events take place, where the only things that "bloom" are "tombstones."

The heavy emphasis on drought and despair is expressed on the cover of the French record sleeve: The drawing by Frank Margerin (a French cartoonist known for his comic strips presenting humorous re-creations of the late fifties and early sixties in France) shows a bottle with an SOS message rolled inside, but the bottle floats on a sea of sand. Only the names of the artists in alphabetical order appear on the front cover of the sleeve; the group picture is on the back, suggesting the differences in priorities and in organization between the "USA For Africa" and "Chanteurs Sans Frontières" records. The American record uses the artists as primary supports for the project because the latter is not in sharp focus. The French record identifies the cause it tries to defend and uses the group; the drawing and the name "Chanteurs Sans Frontières" would suggest Ethiopia and the "Médecins Sans Frontières" already familiar to most Frenchmen and would provide them the needed support.

Both the lyrics of the songs and the way the records were presented to the respective anticipated publics may also be seen as reflecting deeper characteristics pertaining to each people. The lyrics of the American song are more clearly on the idealistic side, dealing with general values, noble sentiments associated with a desire to thoroughly solve the problem through the application of ideals whose reliability is universally admitted (life, love—again harking back to the Beatles' anthem—God, togetherness) but whose practicality may not be so easily demonstrated in a real situation. The lyrics of the French song are more down-to-earth, more sharply focused and filled with evocative images, as if there were a need to convince the listener that the request is truly based upon a situation which demands that action be taken because, if this were not the case, we would watch a world disappear before us and ours may be the next to disappear. These few differences found in two brief songs may reflect some differences between the personalities associated with each national character—the generalized altruism of Americans, the more focused, practical and less altruistic mind of the French, for example.

Both records did nevertheless achieve what had been expected of them. The huge sums raised by "USA For Africa" and "Chanteurs Sans Frontières" did help the causes each group had targeted. The American nevertheless had a loftier goal in mind: not only to raise money but also to raise "awareness" and "change priorities so that everyone's right to live without unnecessary pain and malnutrition or a lack of shelter is guaranteed" (Kragen 5). The founders of "Chanteurs Sans Frontières," however, had always said that their own goals were less ambitious, since the record had been produced only to "cure, feed and save thousand of persons threatened by famine and sickness"[7].

Who Are We Helping? Questions, Reactions and Criticism

There were few criticisms leveled at the American project or at any of its participants; only occasional comments about the "ego-checking" problems of a few performers. There was more criticism in France about the "Chanteurs Sans Frontières" undertaking—about the record, its originators and the ideological slant of the "Médecins Sans Frontières" organization's strange political bedfellows. Some French critics questioned the need for artists to record a hit song in order to raise money for a cause they happened to deem worthy of their own efforts and time. "Why not, instead, give your *own* money and not money earned indirectly through a group's efforts?" was the question of some critics, who went on to suggest that artists might support a cause more quietly and on a more regular basis. (L[ogent] 35). Others questioned the good faith of and the possible hidden political motives behind the "Médecins Sans Frontières" organization, and its associated filial "Liberté Sans

Frontiéres" in particular. The latter, also the brainchild of Brauman, was known as a front for the New Right, whose members were thought to be exploiting the phenomenon in order to increase their following (Logent 39).[8] Others openly questioned the honesty of the organization of some of the groups in charge of the distribution of food and money: food was rumored to have been stolen or sold for profit, some of it was left to rot, transportation was not always correctly planned, and the Ethiopian government was seen as less than reliable when it came to statistics about the populations affected by the famine and their respective needs (J. de B. 7). A few others even hinted at a possible repetition of the sorry turn of events that had marked the Russian famine relief in the twenties and the Cambodian help in the late seventies.

These criticisms did not disappear overnight but were soon overshadowed by another more grandiose project, again owing to Geldof's energies: a huge rock concert to be held on 13 July, 1985, at Wembley Stadium near London, and JFK Stadium, Philadelphia. The two mammoth "Live Aid" concerts would be broadcast worldwide by satellite and were expected to gross at least £10,000,000 for Ethiopia (Barol (b) 53).[9] As soon as the date and the list of potential participants were mentioned, there emerged rumors even more outlandish than those associated with the earlier project. The most tenacious of these had to do with a planned reunion of the three remaining members of the Beatles on the stage of Wembley Stadium, where Paul McCartney was scheduled to close the show. That reunion never materialized, but others, such as the reunion of The Who and that of two former members of Led Zeppelin (Jimmy Page and Robert Plant), did.

The enterprise was vast, even by today's standards: the live television and radio broadcasts on an ad-hoc network required the use of fourteen satellites (compared to the four used during the Olympic Games). The number and stature of the performers also led the organizers to worry about security problems on and around the stages. The American concert opened at nine in the morning with an appeal by Joan Baez. Show highlights appeared in all the media and it was estimated that the effort would raise $50 million in America (Barol & al. 57). A few contretemps did take place and, as innocuous as they may appear, they indicated a change in the perceptions of the "USA For Africa/Live Aid" efforts. First, Huey Lewis backed out of the concert early in July after he expressed questions about whether the money would actually get to Africa to help anybody (Stewart 1D). Others resented Lionel Richie's heavy-handed forcing of artists to come onstage and sing "We Are The World" at the closing of the American concert (Collins 3D). Two sides soon emerged, one advocating solutions involving the United Nations or independent commissions encouraging Africans to become self-sufficient the other advocating the continuation of fund-raising operations in order to help needy people in and out of Africa.[10].

Similar criticisms had already appeared in France: politically-minded questions were raised about the honesty of the fund-raisers, the food distributors and Ethiopian officials, whose degree of corruption could scarcely be overestimated; others criticized the French government for not releasing its military transport planes to help distribute food in remote areas—the French have an air-base in Djibouti (Backman 52). The "Live Aid" effort hardly affected further French efforts for its album was sold in France and, since then, records such as "La faim y en a marre!" [Polygram, PY 102-884522-7] have been produced under the "Live Aid" auspices or under its French branch. The only notable fund-raising effort was organized by Renaud and Coluche in association with French anti-racist groups such as "SOS Racisme" and took place in Paris on 15 June, 1985. "SOS Racisme" became known widely early in 1985, when it launched its famous message: "Touche pas à mon pote!" [Do not touch my buddy!], referring to the upsurge of anti-Arab feelings in France. Half a million spectators attended the concert and helped "SOS Racisme" obtain a better financial foundation ("Feu vert" 16). A parallel effort, related to the charity begins-at-home concept expressed in America by the "Farm Aid" concerts and the "Hands Across America" operation, also developed in France. In order to help feed the homeless and the poor during the winter months, Coluche founded popular restaurants where food was served free to all who asked for it. These "Restaurants du Coeur" received limited financial assistance from the French government but raised most of their food either through repeated calls to the public or direct calls to supermarkets, food distributors and industrialists. Coluche died in June, 1986 in a motorcycle accident and his widow decided to continue his enterprise (Tenaille 179-182).

These criticisms also serve illustrate the differences between the French and Americans. The American effort was organized along idealistic, non-political principles and the funds were channeled through financially "transparent" organizations. The money could always be accounted for and the only possible criticism would have to do with the respective amounts allotted to the various relief organizations. The French project, on the other hand, was more focused but could also lend itself to more intense criticism, owing in part to the extreme-rightist leanings of Brauman and some of the groups he headed. In addition, the presence of anti-racist organizations among the organizers, may have helped exacerbate criticism and attacks from some political circles. Finally, Coluche's efforts in France and the "Farm Aid" movement in the United States could have played a role in the origin of some of the criticisms launched at efforts for people far away while, in each of the countries, there were poor and homeless who needed help.

"USA For Africa" and "Chanteurs Sans Frontières": The Passing of a Fad?

By mid-1986, after having been inspired by Geldof's early attempt, it was already apparent that both France and America had followed truly different paths. Several factors may explain these differences. It has already been mentioned that the two projects had organized following two different patterns. The "Chanteurs Sans Frontières" had, from the very beginning, gathered together for a more focused kind of project, to help "Médecins Sans Frontières." The "USA For Africa" project was more ambitious. The respective names of the projects illustrate this difference: in the American case, the name of the country is featured prominently, suggesting that the tide of support originates not so much from individuals but from the country itself; in the French case, the name suggested an effort of sympathizers to help a particular organization than the effort of an entire nation. here may be another reason for the fact that criticisms of the French project were more vocal—from French quarters—than the American criticism of the U.S. project from within the United States. The difference in the two projects' scope may also have stemmed from linguistic factors, which enable English-speaking artists to become popular in France but make it difficult for any French-speaking performer to gain a sizeable following outside France. Moreover, it is clear that the evolution of each movement was influenced by the cultural and political systems within which they originated.

A few similarities in the evolution of these movements however, also appear. Both had begun by looking outside their respective countries of origin for a noteworthy cause, but gradually more parochial considerations began to come to the fore or potential donors began to wonder whether their money could not be used to help fellow countrymen whose needs were real and pressing. The "Farm Aid" concerts clearly exploited this trend by emphasizing the plight of the American farmer, not only as a key figure in the traditional representation of American civilization and its foundings but also as the one who was producing all those foodstuffs being sent to help the malnourished.

The passing away of a fad was not the only reason why changes occurred in the orientation of fund-raising efforts in both America and in France. Nagging questions relating to the use of money, the actual effects of the millions spent, and the apparent failure to contain famine and drought were constantly raised and never clearly answered. Reports from the field, dismissed lightly at first, began to suggest a pattern of irregularities in the storing, distribution, and accounting for all the aid provided. Those who had given money were beginning to learn that their well-intentioned help had been useful in some regions but had gone for naught in others. Such reports appeared at first in specialized publications but were soon featured in popular magazines as well (Shawcross 67). The pattern of accusations was always the same: enough attention had not been paid to practical details. It also became clear that giving alone was not necessarily the best practical solution because it tended to create either corruption or dependency. But, when some of the criticisms by representatives of the groups working in Ethiopia became too sharply worded, the Ethiopian government, some of whose members had been said to have profited from the aid, simply forced the group out.

The case of "Médecins Sans Frontières" provides a vivid illustration of both the Ethiopian government's attitude and also a clear view of the inner workings of many such humanitarian associations. "Médecins Sans Frontières" began to express frustration at the attitude of the Ethiopian government vis-à-vis two problems: the starving of those who lived in regions where independent groups were at odds with the Mengistu government and the forceful relocation of populations into newly created villages. The result was that, on 2 December, 1985, the Ethiopian government demanded that "Médecins Sans Frontières" leave the country. In its order, the Ethiopian government did not try to address any of the criticisms but instead accused the group of stealing money from the assistance funds. No other relief group working in Ethiopia at the time reacted to this expulsion. This episode was discussed at length in two books published in France late in 1986 (Gluckman and Wolton, Ruggin). Some actions by the Ethiopian government were also seen as unfeeling or at least poorly timed, such as the spending of more than half a million dollars to build a swimming-pool and a recreation room in the Ethiopian U.N. Mission building in Geneva ("LeMonde" 57).

Even Geldof was said to be tired of critics carping about his group's disbursement of famine relief funds (Peisch 2D). Nobody suspected him of misusing the funds, but he was still perceived as being partly to blame for mistakes of the organization. However his nomination for the Nobel Prize underscored the many positive feelings expressed in his favor, as did his receiving an honorary knighthood in July, 1986 (Fricke 25). By the end of 1986, Geldof was back to music full-time and was attempting to regain his status in the world of entertainment, but not before he wrote the history of his involvement with the hunger in Africa (Geldof *passim*). The spending plan and the total amounts available were released by the "Live Aid Foundation" and the "Band Aid Trust" in February, 1986. Out of the $92.1 million available from the concerts and recordings, 20% had been committed to emergency relief, 20% to logistical support, and 60% to long-term projects $34 million had already been spent and $58.1 million were left to be spent (Mac Neil 7).

The Future of Popular Music Altruism

It appears that the millions raised will be sorely needed in forthcoming years. During 1986 there was a dramatic drop in governmental and private contributions to relief organizations both in France and in the United States. Several reasons may be inferred: the appearance of new causes (AIDS in particular both in France and in the United States); the emergence of a new famine crisis in Ethiopia, along with violence from revolutionary groups (Brand 39); and the progressive lack of interest for a cause rapidly fading from the headlines. In France, "SOS Racisme" has been facing monetary problems since 1986 ("SOS Racisme en perdition" 4), and in America the "Farm Aid" concerts have been abandoned (de Curtis 38).

It may safely be said that the "USA For Africa," the "Chanteurs Sans Frontières," and the "Live Aid" concert suggest the different orientation in American and French society towards entertainment and engagement, towards the political and the ideological, and towards pragmatism and altruism. These phenomena may demonstrate that the solution to solve hunger or homelessness is too serious to be left merely to the popular culture industry, which in the West is geared for profit, not philanthropy.

Notes

[1] For a more detailed description of the project, see the "Special Pull Out Section" devoted to the project in *USA Today*, 20 September, 1985.

[2] For an example of this ad see page 170 of the January, 1975, issue of *L'autre Journal Les Nouvelles Littéraires*.

[3] Among other records whose royalties were targeted for helping hunger in Africa, one could find, by the end of 1986, at least half a dozen items in addition to those already mentioned in this essay. They were: "Do something Now," by Gospel singers under the name CAUSE (Christian Artists United to Save the Earth); "Cantare, Cantaras," by Latin stars including Cecilia Cruz, Jose Feliciano and Julio Iglesias; "Stars", with hard-rock performers such as Judas Priest, Iron Maiden and Quiet Riot among others; "Let's Make Africa Green Again," by several British reggae Musicians; "Don't Let Africa Starve," by older rythm-and-blues performers, including former members of the Drifters, the Robins, and the Marvelettes among others; "Warum?" by Austrian rock and pop performers; "Nack im Wind," by German popular performers; "Tears Are Not Enough," by the Canadian All Stars, and "Keep Them Alive," by Jazz to Fund Hunger—a group of about fifty jazz notables.

[4] The project finally raised more than $10 million.

[5] None of the pages of Breslin's book is numbered.

[6] Renaud's letter appeared in *Libération* [Paris, France], 3 June, 1985, on page 37.

[7] Mentioned in Renaud's letter, cf. note above.

[8] For a more extensive treatment of the New Right attempts, see the May 1985, issue of *Le Monde Diplomatique* [Paris, France].

[9] For a detailed presentation of the "Live Aid" project, see, for example, the special 15 August, 1985, issue of *Rolling Stone*. The total "Live Aid" contribution was about $70,000,000.

[10]Pro and con examples may be found in the 17 July, 1985, opinion page of *USA Today*.

Bibliography

"Aid to Africa."*The Economist*, July 20, 1985: 29-32.

Backman, René. "Mort sans crédit en Ethiopie."*Le Nouvel Observateur* [Paris, France], May 31-June 6, 1985: 52-53.

Barol, Bill. (a) "I Ain't Gonna Play Sun City." *Newsweek*, October 28, 1985: 94-95.

——— (b)"Newsmakers." *Newsweek*, June 24, 1985: 53.

——— et al. "Rock Around the World." *Newsweek*, July 22, 1985: 56-58.

Brand, David. "Twin Plagues of War and Famine." *Time*, March 28, 1988: 39-40.

Breslin, David. *We Are The World*. New York: Putnam/Perigee Books, 1985.

"Bringing the Hunger Fight Home." *Newsweek*, February 10, 1986: 46.

Collins, Monica. " 'Live Aid' A High Tech High at Home." *USA Today*, 15 July, 1985: 3D.

Cooper, Nancy, with Steven Strasser. "Chernobyl: Account No. 904." *Newsweek*, June 9, 1986: 36.

de B., J. "L'aide internationale aux victimes de la famine. Démentis et mises au point." *Le Monde* [Paris, France], 11 June, 1985: 7.

de Curtis, Anthony, "Willie Nelson: Farm Aid II a 'Success.' Farm Aid III May be Postponed Until Next Year." *Rolling Stone*, August 28, 1986: 38.

"Dealers Cheer 'World' Album." *Billboard*, April 20, 1985: 1.

"Famine: Bob Geldof se moque do l'ONU." *Libération* [Paris, France], 31 May - 1 June 1986: 28.

"Feu Vert: Harlem Désir." *L'Express*, June 28, 1985: 16.

Fricke, David "For Geldof: The Biggest Price of All." *Rolling Stone*, August 29, 1985: 25.

Gates, David. "Farm Aid." *Rolling Stone*, November 2, 1985: 24-28, 67, 69.

Geldof, Bob. *Is That It?* New York: Weidenfield & Nicholson, 1987.

"Geldof's Newest Game: Sport Aid." *USA Today*, 6 March 1986: 2D.

Glucksman, André, and Thierry Wolton. *Silence on tue*. Paris: Grasset, 1986.

Goodman, Fred. "USA for Africa 'Authorizing' Dealers. Crackdown on Counterfeit Merchandise Intensifies."*Billboard*, May 4, 1985: 22.

Grein, Paul. (a) "Chart Beat." *Billboard*, May 11, 1985: 6.

——— (b) "Ethiopia-Aid Single, Video Take Off." *Billboard*, January 5, 1985: 3.

——— (c) "46 US Acts Team for New Aid Single." *Billboard*, February 9, 1985: 1, 69.

——— (d) "Richie Enlists US Superstars. Acts Battle Africa Hunger." *Billboard*, January 19, 1985: 1, 75.

Hellmich, Nancy, & al. "A Shower of Good Will, Good Times." *USA Today*. 23 September 1985: 1D, 2D.

Kragen, Ken. "An Open Letter to Everyone in Radio." *Billboard*, March 8, 1985: 5.

"Le Monde." *Le Point* [Paris, France], June 3, 1985: 57.

"L'Ethiopie se meurt. Vous lui devez 46 Francs."*L'Autre Journal. Les Nouvelles Littéraires* [Paris, France], January 1985: 170.

L[ogent], P[ascal]. "Faim du monde." *Rock and Folk* [Paris, France], June, 1985: 35.

Logent, Pascal. "LSF appelle MSF." *Liberation* [Paris, France], 8-9 June, 1985: 39.

MacNeil, Scott. "Live Aid: Getting and Giving." *Newsweek*, February 10, 1986: 7.

"Manifestation anti-raciste. Un concert á la 'Woodstock' a rassemblé 400 000 jeunes Francais." *Journal Francais d'Amérique*, August 2-15 1985: 2.

Miller, Jim. "Brother Can You Spare a Song?" *Newsweek*, October, 28, 1985: 94-95.

"Millions Starving. Donations Dry Up." *The [Scranton, PA] Sunday Times*, 17 August, 1986: 1A.

O'Connor, Colleen. "Hands Across America." *Newsweek*, May 19, 1986: 25.

Peisch, Jeffrey. "Geldof Has Had It With Live Aid Guff." *USA Today*, 25 November, 1985: 2D.

Potel, Jean-Yves, ed. *L'état de la France et de ses habitants*. Paris: Editions de la Découverte, 1985.

Prévos, André. (a)"CBers and cibistes: The Development and Impact of CB Radio in France." *Journal of Popular Culture* 19.1 (1986): 145-154.

———— (b)"The CLARB and Soul Bag." *The Black Perspective in Music* 15.2 (1987): 243-257.

"Quand Coluche dribble entre l'Ethiopie et Bruxelles." *Libération* [Paris, France, 3 June, 1985: 44.

"Queen to Honor Geldof." *International Herald Tribune*, 12 July, 1986: 18.

"Ram Dam pour l'Ethiopie." *Libération* [Paris, France], 16 May, 1985: 24.

"Reflet des ventes." *Libération* [Paris, France], 22 May 1985: 32.

Rioux, Lucien. "Show-biz et fraternité." *Le Nouvel Observateur* [Paris, France], June 14-20, 1985: 74.

Ruffin, Jean-Christophe. *Le piège*. Paris: Lattès, 1986.

"Samedi 15." *Actuel* [Paris, France], June 1985: 141.

Scheurs, Fred. "Music Q & A: Little Steven." *Rolling Stone*, January 16, 1986: 17.

Shawcross, William. "Report from Ethiopia. While Food Rots on the Dock, Thousands are Starving." *Rolling Stone*, July 18-August 6, 1985: 67.

"SOS Racisme en perdition." *Journal Français d'Amérique*, February 28-March 3, 1986: 4.

"Special Pull-Out Section: Farm Aid." *USA Today*, 20 September 1985: 5D-8D.

"Special Report: U.K...Newsline..." *Billboard*, January 12, 1985: 9.

Stein, Sylvaine. "Coluche père nourricier." *L'Express. Edition Internationale*, January 10, 1986: 36.

Stewart, Sally Ann. "Huey Lewis is Out of Live Aid." *USA Today*, 2 July, 1985: 1D.

"Tchernobyl Aid." *Libération* [Paris, France], 31 May-June, 1986: 35.

Tenaille, Frank. *Coluche* Paris: Editions Seghers, 1986.

Ware, Ethlie-Ann "USA For Africa Project Growing." *Billboard*, March 30, 1985: 4.

"We Are The World. Special Issue." *Billboard* April 6, 1985.

Wilkinson, Ray. "How to Help Africa Help Itself." *Newsweek* June 9, 1986: 39.

Yonnet, Paul. *Jeux. modes et masses. La société française et le moderne. 1945-1985*. Paris: Gallimard, 1985.

Zecchini, Laurent. "Les organisations humanitaires en Ethiopie: Témoins ou complices?" *Le Monde* [Paris, France], 25 July, 1986: 1, 3.

Zimmerman, David. "The Outlaw Uses Music to Get Justice." *USA Today,* 10 September 1985: 1D, 2D.

Appendix

"We Are The World"
Written by Michael Jackson and Lionel Richie. All Rights Reserved. Copyright 1985. Mijac Music (BMI) and Brockman Music (ASCAP).

There comes a time when we heed a certain call
When the world must come together as one
The people are dying
And it's time to lend a hand to life
The greatest gift of all.

CHORUS   We are the world, we are the children
          We are the ones who make a brighter day
          So let's start giving
          There's a choice we're making'
          We're saving our own lives
          It's true we'll make a better day
          Just you and me.

BRIDGE   (Michael Jackson solo)   When you're down and out
          (Huey Lewis solo)   There seems no hope at all
          (Cyndi Lauper solo)   But if you just believe there's no
          (Kim Carnes solo)   way we can fall
          (Kim and Huey duet)   Let us realize that a change
                                    can only come
                                    When we stand together as one.

FILLS
          Bob Dylan
          Bruce Springstein
          Ray Charles.

"Ethiopie"
Written by Renaud Séchan, with Frank Langloff. All Rights Reserved. Copyright
1985
SACEM

ls n'ont jamais vu la pluie	They have never seen the rain,
lls ne savent même plus sourire	They no longer know how to smile,
lls n'y a même plus de larmes	There are no longer any tears
Dans leurs yeux si grands	In their eyes so wide.
Les enfants d'Ethiopie	The children of Ethiopia,
Embarqués sur un navire	Embarked on a ship
Qui n'a plus ni voiles ni rames	Without sails or oars,
Attendent le vent	Await the wind

REFRAIN:

Loin du coeur et loin des yeux	Away from the heart and from the eyes,
De nos villes de nos banlieues	From our cities, our suburbs,
L'Ethiopie meurt peu à peu	Ethiopia dies slowly,
Peu à peu	Slowly.
Rien qu'une chanson pour eux	Only a song or them
Pour ne plus fermer les yeux	To stop closing our eyes,
C'est beaucoup et c'est bien peu	That's a lot and that's very little,
C'est bien peu	Very little.

(Transliteration: André J.M. Prévos)

Part III:
Popular Culture as Common Ground

—*"Tubing out" in the U.S.S.R. and the U.S.A.*

—*Comparative popular culture as a teaching tool*

And Now, He-e-e-e-re's Misha!: Soviet Television Since *Perestroika*

Alexandra Heidi Karriker

The divergence between Soviet and American television has narrowed in the later eighties as "glasnost" (openness) and "perestroika" (restructuring) have had their impact on the "blue screen," as TV is called in the USSR. There have been many changes in the format and variety of Soviet programs, the broadcast day has been lengthened, and many new shows have been added. These modifications clearly reflect a Westernization in television programming that has resulted in more viewer access and a greater utilization of the medium.

An unprecedented dynamism has energized Soviet television as studio audiences and home viewers are asked to respond to inquiries about the availability of specific goods, the worthiness of services rendered, and the general quality of life under reconstructive reforms. On-location shooting for TV has increased; for example, General Secretary Gorbachev's frequent on-the-street conversations with random passers-by are being featured regularly on the news.

The new Soviet policy of candidness is reflected in all types of programs, from newscasts to talk shows, and by increased attention to compelling social issues such as alcoholism, drug abuse, or worker incompetence. Now official viewpoints are questioned; for example, economic problems are attacked head-on, often with the participation of viewers through on-air call-ins. As Soviet television shows have become more timely and relevant to contemporary life, they have become more popular with the public. Soviet programming has in fact become more interesting—more interesting, perhaps, than network television in the United States.

As access to events in the West, particularly in America, is increasing for the Soviet people, an impressive mass communication campaign is bringing television into the homes of its citizens from the Baltic to Vladivostok, an area so vast that it spans eleven time zones and contains one sixth of the earth's land area. A massive system of satellites allows the transmission of television throughout the fifteen Soviet republics. There are eleven major television centers in the Soviet Union besides the main studios in Moscow. In addition, there are forty-four regional studios from Abakan, in Soviet Central Asia, to Yaroslavl, in the Russian republic. Whereas in 1953 there were only 225,000 television sets and merely 27 million in 1969, there are now 85 million sets in Soviet homes, and this number is growing rapidly. In 1983, when there were 308 television sets per 1,000 population in the USSR, there were 790 per 1,000 in the United States. Color broadcasts began regularly in 1967 in the Soviet Union; approximately 20,000 color sets were in use by 1971, and now there are 12 million color sets.[1] The production of 10-11 million television sets annually is projected by 1990.[2]

Whereas television in the United States is, of course, privately owned and operated (except for PBS), Soviet television is state-owned, state-controlled, and virtually non-commercial. "Gosteleradio," the State Committee for Television and Radio, oversees the content, structure and distribution of programming. In America, on the other hand, the FCC grants licenses to stations, most of them members of the National Association of Broadcasters, which sets guidelines for news and commercials, but does not monitor individual channels.

America's viewing habits have been shaped for four decades by the visual imagery of sponsored TV programming. Consigned a commercial role from its inception, most American television is designed to lure advertising revenue and audiences to whom the "pitch" can be made. Soviet television, however, has developed from a political propaganda tool to a mass access medium through which socio-political and cultural goals, utilizing techniques pioneered in the West, are disseminated.

National programs in the USSR originate in the Ostankino television studios and other facilities in Moscow, which transmit five channels. Selected programs from the two Soviet national networks, "Programma I" and "Programma II" are relayed via satellite with time shifts, so that the broadcast day begins uniformly, and the news program, "Vremya" (Time), is aired at 9:00 p.m. local time, throughout the country. In addition, district television centers provide regional programming, which is also becoming more creative.

Today on Soviet TV

The television day in the USSR begins with a colorful test pattern. Then, between 6:30 and 8:30 a.m. on "Programma II," the "blue screen" comes alive with the stretches, jumps and contortions of slender young aerobics instructors who effortlessly, and with a smile, do their routines to the blithe rhythms of live piano accompaniment. Dressed in stylishly revealing leotards, the leader curtly and professionally describes the steps, without explicitly resorting to sexual innuendo through glances or body movements. Camera angles are also discreet. But such decorum does not diminish the popularity of the show: it is especially favored by male viewers. A similar "Rhythmical Gymnastics" program, but to the syncopation of rock music, is a frequent late-evening entertainment. This show, however, is more overtly sensual, as the girls (and a few men— dance in the recording studio, or on location at the beach or in the woods. The aerobics and jazz dancing may be intercut with Western videos of surfers and water skiers. Comparable shows on American television, like the "Twenty-minute Workout," are presented on the VHF channels or on PBS stations because titillation is readily available in regular programming.

Exercise programs, undoubtedly aimed at instruction and physical fitness, probably provide more entertainment value than calisthenics for a good many viewers. And shows such as these exemplify the dilemma embracing Soviet television; on the one hand, authorities stress that the instructional, informative and ideological functions of all programs must be evident; yet, on the other hand, viewers have been shown time and again to watch television primarily for entertainment purposes.[3]

Unlike commercial American television, Soviet TV does not sell products, unless we view official ideology as a product. But during this period of reform, there is less propaganda and more information about world events, which seemingly has increased the amount of time people spend watching television. Although the Soviets do not have a system comparable to the Nielsen ratings, successful programming is measured by the amount of mail the stations receive. Recent articles in *Literaturnaya gazeta (Literary Gazette)* attest to the overwhelming popularity of some of the new presentations, including "90 Minutes," a variety show, which was lengthened to two hours after enormous viewer response.[4]

"Programma I" broadcasts some of the more innovative talk, music, and news shows. Its programs can be summarized as follows: morning information/music show; sports, films, 5-15 minute news breaks; cartoons, documentaries, natural science programs; international news (15 min.), political and philosophical discussions; national network news (usually 40 minutes to an hour in duration), analysis of "perestroika" (10 min.); music, theatre, film. On Friday evenings there is a late night talk show, "Vzglyad" (Viewpoint). Sunday programming, which begins with the news at 8:00 a.m., not at 6:30 (the sign-on time for the rest of the week), includes a half-hour overview of sports.

"Programma II" follows this same general pattern: morning gymnastics, music, documentaries; foreign language study (Italian, French, German, Spanish, and English); science and nature programs, films; 5-15 minute news breaks; lectures and interviews; sports; poetry readings and commentaries on literature; a children's bedtime program, "Good Night, Little Ones!" which utilizes puppets and clay and sand animation (at around 8:00 p.m.); a five-minute public service announcement; network news and critiques of "perestroika;" films, concerts, sports.

Soviet television fare includes feature, animated, and documentary films and made-for-television serials. The natural science programs often stress ecological perspectives; the cartoons and children's bedtime show usually impart a moral. Symphony, jazz and folk music concerts are presented live more often than not and in their entirety. "Vremya" (Time), the national news, sports and weather program, is signed for the deaf on one of the channels. It occupies a constant time slot, 9:00 p.m. Thus films or other programs may be interrupted by the presentation of the news. Telecasts can begin at any 5-minute interval. American viewers would notice the plethora of educational and cultural programs, the distinct lack of soap operas and situational comedies, and a paucity of purely escapist productions.

In general, Soviet television programs bear more similarity to the type of shows aired on American PBS stations and on European TV networks than on the major American channels. In addition, the number of programs devoted to actual instruction calls forth the comparison with cable television stations associated with universities. Although the pedagogical programs on "Programma I" and "Programma II" do not carry course credit, they may be used by educational institutions, as are the programs on the Moscow educational channel. Thus, Soviet television combines programming which in America is assigned to public, private (cable) and educational networks.

A listing of the day's programs appears at the start and close of the broadcast day and before any long breaks, which often occur from 12-3 p.m. on "Programma I," and between 4 and 5:30 p.m. on "Programma II." Infrequently, programming is supplemented by irregularly scheduled five-or ten-minute public service announcements, which promote such items as the state lottery, or which urge viewers to use water sparingly. Programs are repeated on the same channel, sometimes even during the same day, as in the case of language or science classes. If aired first on "Programma I," and deemed highly successful, shows may be repeated on "Programma II," with a time lag of several weeks or even months.

Although many Soviet programs may seem dry, dull or tedious to a Western sensibility, there is considerable variety in the two main television channels, "Programma I" and "Programma II." Moscow has a separate local channel which broadcasts from 6:45 p.m. to midnight, an evening educational channel, and the Leningrad channel. Other cities do not have such a wide choice. For example, Stavropol, the birthplace of Gorbachev at the northern foot of the Caucasus Mountains, with a population of approximately 300,000, has only the two main channels available, with local programming sandwiched in during the broadcast day.

(Soviet) TV Guide

The educational orientation of Soviet television is apparent in programs as diverse as prime time newscasts, documentary films, a few game shows (which are aimed at teaching a lesson of some kind), cartoons, and variety shows, which often feature folk musical ensembles and stand-up comics. American program categories are less fluid and reflect a clearer delineation of informative broadcasts such as National Geographic Specials or journalistic "White Papers" from situational comedies such as "The Cosby Show" and "Family Ties."

Soviet television shows are puritanical in comparison with American programs. There is a noticeable lack of sex, nudity, and profanity, but these elements are creeping into the broadcasting via Western videos. There is violence in the Soviet war films, and the cruel treatment of women and children is evident, especially in movies dealing with the minorities. In American TV, on the other hand, sex, violence and vulgar language are no longer confined to late-night programming, or even to films and videos. Geraldo Rivera's latest features, which have been relegated to the category of "Trash TV" by some critics, are not unique in their emphasis on the lugubrious, the kinky, or the suggestive.[5]

On Soviet TV, there are still many "talking heads;" newscasters often read from texts held at waist level into one of two microphones on the desk. Programs, however, are not tied into a rigid time slot, except for "Vremya," the news. There are often long pauses between programs and there can be several hours during the day when a channel may not broadcast at all; during these periods either a test pattern or the time (to the second) is shown on the screen.

On "Programma I," a two-hour talk/video/commentary show, "120 Minutes," begins at 6:30 a.m. This program is presented by several hosts who field call-ins and do on-the-street interviewing. The emcees' critically perceptive remarks or scathing indictments of a variety of problems have boosted them to a level of stardom previously unfamiliar to this medium in the USSR. The tempo of "120 Minutes" approaches that of American programs of similar content, like the "Today" show or "Late Night with David Letterman." The intercutting of segments showcasing international and local musicians sustains the pace and variety of the presentation. The format for such programs indicates that the Soviets are finally realizing the potential of television to do more than provide position papers or conspicuous propaganda.

Studio interviews have been a mainstay on Soviet television for years. In the past, the programs were stiffly formal, with the ideology primarily reflecting Communist party policy and the "conversation" amounting to little more than a voicing of prescribed views from prepared scripts. "Glasnost" has permitted a more intimate format, with the commentators carrying on spontaneous dialogues with interviewees as they probe controversial topics in the style of Dick Cavett or William F. Buckley. Soviet talk shows have gained tremendous popularity, and the chatty, personal views of talk show hosts are emerging as they develop their own media personae and achieve celebrity status. Urmas Ott's program, "Television Acquaintance," shown once a month on Estonian TV, regularly draws the highest viewer response, even though it is aired infrequently by American standards.[6]

The sounds of Soviet television have changed markedly; more rock music is heard, and punk and heavy metal groups, such as "Aquarium" and "Bravo," which just a few years ago would have been labeled 'decadent' and banned, now perform frequently on variety shows. European and American music videos are shown on talk shows such as "Viewpoint," on dance and exercise programs such as "Rythmic Gymnastics," and curiously, as a backdrop to superimposed reports of weather conditions throughout the republics of the USSR. The program "What, Where, and When?" had developed an ingenious format for using rock videos. One episode of the show demarcates sixty seconds, the amount of time that viewers have to guess what is occurring in a jarring, rapid-cut Millie Jackson and Elton John video, "War," which viewers identify as portraying the vicissitudes of married life.

Through "Glasnost," Darkly

The West is no longer shrouded in mystery for the average Soviet citizen since the visibility of things American is on the rise—from interviews with American families who watched The Turner Network broadcasts of live Soviet television, to the airing of programs that originate in America, such as the four-part series, "A Portrait of the Soviet Union." Simulcasts of the "Spacebridges," satellite link-ups of studio audiences in Boston/Leningrad and Seattle/ Leningrad, were co-hosted by Phil Donahue and Soviet journalist Vladimir Pozner. The "Capitol to Capitol" series featured live debates between American congressmen and government representatives from the Supreme Soviet. Channels in the USSR broadcast these programs complete with the American commercials, which gave viewers an unprecedented opportunity to see Americans in their own milieu of business conglomerates, fast food, kitchen gadgets, and personal toiletries.

Such programming represents a drastic departure from the time (in the not-so-distant-past) when the news was read by actors, not journalists, from stories supplied by TASS. When shows were being prepared, news scripts were meticulously scrutinized and edited for ideological concerns before broadcasting.

Gorbachev's new economic policies have resulted in a cultural revolution in many areas akin to the "thaws" brought on by the relaxation of censorship during Khrushchev's leadership. Nabokov's novels are being serialized in Soviet journals, and Pasternak's *Doctor Zhivago* has finally been made available to the very people who were meant to be its first readers when it won the Nobel Prize for Literature thirty years ago. There is a barrage of absorbing, long-suppressed prose in Soviet magazines, such as *Ogonek* and *Novy mir,* and in newspapers such as *Literaturnaya gazeta, Pravda,* and *Izvestia.* Controversial topics are now the norm, rather than the exception, as any single issues will reveal. The October 12, 1988 edition of *Literaturnaya gazeta,* for example, included lengthy articles about the following controversial topics: Claude Lanzmann's "Shoah," a nine-hour documentary of the Holocaust; Andrei Konchalovsky's film, "Asya's Happiness," which was completed in 1966 and only made available for internal distribution in 1988; a story about a young Estonian who left a life of drugs in the city to take up farming on a small plot of land; and a feature on the proliferation of teen gangs.[7]

The changes which the media have undergone in the past two years are also reflected in the quality and content of programs on Soviet TV, many of which deal with things American. Vladimir Dunaev, Soviet correspondent for TASS in Washington, has provided interviews with Americans on the street and in their homes. One notable report concerned the Discovery Channel's presentation of 55 hours of Soviet television via satellite and an interview with the Gilman Family in the suburbs of Washington about their reaction to the programs. Another was an interview with Kris Christopherson after the airing of the ABC mini-series, "Amerika."

Television has lifted some of the stifling folds of the Iron Curtain through the propitious dissemination of news and cultural developments worldwide. As it is being used by the present administration, the medium also provides more of a forum for true mass-communication. Because television requires no direct physical link other than a receiver, it has succeeded in making an array of informational and cultural events available to even the most rural and least educated population.

The Stalin era, shrouded in silence for thirty-five years since the dictator's death, has often been cited as an example of the ability of the Soviet political machinery to shape and select the depiction of historical events to meet the needs of the Communist Party. But now, within the Kremlin of Mikhail Gorbachev, even the Cult of Personality is no longer a taboo topic in the USSR, as exposés appear in the press, as docudramas about the mistakes of earlier years are aired on national television, and as films such as Abuladze's "Repentance" and novels such as Rybakov's *Children of the Arbat* are released. This does not imply, of course, that there are no more subjects forbidden to the media; rather, it shows a shifting perspective and more tolerance for non-dogmatic views.

On the other hand, libraries were recently ordered to remove books giving pre-Gorbachev views, as a librarian from the Crimea complained to the newspaper *Izvestia* in a letter: "So it turns out that, even as we open up the archive materials of a half-century ago, we are creating new 'blank spots' in our very recent history."[8] Will this administration resort to earlier tactics in the name of "new thinking?" If libraries are undergoing such censorship, how will television be affected? Undoubtedly the prospects of Soviet TV are very much tied to the political future of Mikhail Gorbachev.

In the television program, "The Process," which is a part of the series entitled "The Revolution Continues," oldtimers who joined the Communist Party in 1917 are interviewed on Red Square about their opinions of the years of Stalin's terror. The interviewer's penetrating questions and the candid answers of the veterans, expressing the doubts and faith of a nation, show the real process of reconstruction that is occurring in the Soviet Union today, not only of economic policies, but of history. And television is bringing these events to the nation.

This time of more open probing for an accurate representation of events during Stalin's regime has brought a great deal of soul-searching and not a little wariness to the attitudes of young people who did not live through those times and do not remember the proverbial midnight knock on the door. Disillusioned by what they see as adult hypocrisy, Soviet adolescents face problems similar to those of their Western peers. More television programs are devoted to teenagers and their predicaments, such as the stresses of studies, conflict with parents, the pressure to get married, "tuning out" through drugs or rock/punk/heavy metal music, or membership in street or motorcycle gangs. In the quite recent past, delinquency and anti-social behavior were banished to the dark areas of Communist society and were not officially acknowledged by the media.

The new period of openness on Soviet television has prompted programs that attempt to deal with wide-spread crime, alcoholism and drug addiction. Many recent Soviet feature films have tackled these problems head-on, among them "Is It Easy to Be Young?", and "Hello, Elena Sergeevna!" The TV documentary "The Second Round" provides interviews with dope addicts and their parents, with poppy growers and doctors. Such surprisingly frank discussions on this program and on other shows like "The Twelfth Floor" and "Moscow Meridian" demonstrate that television programmers are finally attacking the problems of youth and maturity, and are no longer ignoring the "unspeakable" taboos.

The problems of individual national groups have not in the past been treated objectively in the Soviet media. The recent demonstrations in the Baltic republics and the altercations between the Armenians and Azerbaijanies attest to the existence of perplexing issues for which no easy solutions can be found. Bill Keller, who writes in the *New York Times* about the Independent Popular Front of Estonia, which held its first congress in October 1988, entitles his report, "It Used to Be Sedition; Now It's on Estonian TV."[9] This group is advocating the printing of Estonian money, which would have the value of hard currency, and the replacement of state-run collective farms by private agriculture, among other things. Not only was this congress officially sanctioned, but reportedly it was televised as well. As the debate goes on, the events of Baltic unrest continue to be featured on television. This in itself is an indication of significant policy change with regard to what is reported and what is ignored.

Even though there is a distinct absence of religious programming on Soviet television, during May and June of 1988, many shows were devoted to the celebration of the millennium of the Christianization of Russia. Perhaps there was a calculated reason that these programs coincided with the Moscow Summit; however, there have also been other references to the religious heritage of the Soviet Union. For example, the documentary film, "More Light," which aired on "Programma II" on April 5, 1988, described the destruction of magnificent cathedrals, such as that of the Church of Christ the Savior in Moscow. Nevertheless, it is highly unlikely that televangelism or the equivalent of PTL will ever find a place in the USSR's television industry.

Among controversial films which have reached audiences through television is Gleb Panfilov's film, "Theme," completed in 1979 but immediately shelved for eight years. Under Gorbachev, the film was accorded a very limited theatrical run and then was also shown on national television (October 10, 1987). The story involves a disillusioned dramatist experiencing writer's block who travels to the countryside in winter for creative renewal. There he meets a young Jewish tour guide and translator of French whose boyfriend has just applied for an exit visa to Israel. This poignant film portrays the depression and anguish of the Jewish characters with a sensitivity and insight rarely allowed expression before "glasnost."

The problems of inadequate food supplies, and the proliferation of black market profiteering are also attacked in the press and on television. Gorbachev's campaign to eradicate drunkenness has not moved forward as quickly as many had hoped, although it is given much media coverage in the news analysis programs, in public service announcements, and in satirical cartoons.

New programs which have been added recently include several that might fit the label, "Tabloid TV." "Projector perestroika" ("Spotlight on Perestroika") involves analytical reporting to ferret out the production of inferior goods or the delivery of inadequate services.[10] For example, on December 15, 1987, the program considered letters from viewers about diverse topics such as the obstacles to receiving "putyovki" (vacation passes) for health spas, as well as the inability of a factory to pack dishes so that they arrive intact after shipment to stores. In addition, the announcer reported on previous questions discussed on the show and what had been done to provide solutions. Workers, managers, union bosses, party officials and government leaders are interviewed by the reporters whose investigative techniques bespeak a determination to get to the root of the problem and to provide incentive for its quick remedy.

The program, "Dlia vsekh i dlia kazhdogo" ("For One and All"), has a more extensive format and features in-depth looks at serious shortcomings. The October 1, 1987 program dealt with the abominable condition of a new building which had holes between the wall and floor, through which water and snow seeped. The residents filled up the holes with bundles of rags, which in turn become drenched. The reporter was shunted from one office to another in his attempt to find the person responsible for the deplorable construction. But a foreman at the factory commented, "The apartments aren't guaranteed." Arguably, there is more such consumer advocacy on Soviet TV now than there ever has been on American television.

At the end of these programs the address of the television station is given and viewers are encouraged to submit their comments and requests—something rarely done on American TV. Their queries are solicited after other programs as well, and stations receive much correspondence, not all of it positive. Some viewers have reacted with indignation at the muck-raking and fault-finding of the media; they feel that such investigations lower morale and self-esteem.[11]

Public service announcements, which are often ecologically oriented, are aired as sporadically on Soviet TV as they are on American television. They urge viewers to conserve water or electricity or to open savings accounts. But advertisements for consumer items, such as specific brands of motorcycles or watches, are bringing a new American style commercialism to Soviet television. Recent agreements with a U.S. firm to start marketing McDonald's and Pepsi (the Michael Jackson commercials) on Soviet TV will, of course, bring hard currency to Gosteleradio.

What lies ahead for Soviet television programming remains to be seen. For example, will the lure of the advertising dollar or ruble expose the Soviet people to all the hype that American viewers must endure? There is even talk of fostering competition among the channels, as Lidiya Polskaya proposes in *Literaturnaya gazeta*, a move that might promote additional program creativity.[12] For better or worse, these new developments may diminish the gap between American and Soviet television still more.

Notes

[1]*World Radio Television Handbook 1986*, Vol. 40, p. 413; Gayle Durham Hollander, *Soviet Political Indoctrination: Developments in Mass Media and Propaganda Since Stalin*, (New York: 1972), pp. 102-103; *1987 Information Please Almanac*, (New York: 1987).

[2]Ellen Propper Mickiewicz, *Split Signals: Television and Politics in the Soviet Union*, (New York: 1988), p. 3.

[3]James W. Markham, *Voices of the Red Giants: Communications in Russia and China*, (Ames: 1967); Mark W. Hopkins, *Mass Media in the Soviet Union*, (New York: 1970); Ellen Propper Mickiewicz, *Media and the Russian Public*, (New York: 1981).

[4]See John Kohan, "Late Night With Alex and Dima," *Time*, 10 October 1988, p. 68.

[5]See the title story in *Newsweek*, 14 November 1988.

[6]"Piercing the Privacy Veil," *Time*, 10 October 1988, p. 68.

[7]*Literaturnaya gazeta*, 12 October 1988, pp. 15, 8, 12, and 13, respectively.

[8]Quoted in Bill Keller, "Soviet Libraries Purge Books Giving Pre-Gorbachev Views," *New York Times*, 17 August 1988, pp. 1 and A6.

[9]*New York Times*, 3 October 1988, p. 6.

[10]"Projector perestroiki" aired initially on 31 August 1987.

[11]Mickiewicz, *Op. Cit.* (1988), p. 216.

[12]Kohan, *Op. Cit.*, p. 68.

Rocky IV Meets La Grande Illusion: Pedagogy and Theory in Popular Culture Study

Christine Anne Holmlund

Students, teachers, critics and theorists of American and European popular culture and mass media inevitably encounter pejorative categorizations of popular culture as the seamy underside of "Art." Mass media products, including popular films, are commonly regarded as nothing more than entertainment vehicles or commercial ventures, unworthy of serious analysis. Within the United States, the fact that the overwhelming majority of foreign films in distribution are "art" or "auteur" films encourages some critics and audience members to view European films as "cinema" and thus "art," while American films are seen as "movies" and thus "trash."

European theorists and audiences, too, frequently speak disdainfully of Hollywood films, even while attending them in droves. Among European national cinemas, French films in particular benefit from what Pierre Bourdieu terms "the particularity of the French tradition, namely, the persistence, through different epochs and political regimes, of the aristocratic model of 'court society,' personified by a Parisian haute bourgeoisie which...has no counterpart elsewhere, at least for the arrogance of its cultural judgements...—and [which]...has never ceased to exert a sort of fascination in the 'Anglo-Saxon' world, even beyond the circle of snobs and socialites...."[1]

But the too facile labelling of one text as "art" and another as "trash" inhibits appreciation of the extent to which individual films may be compared and impedes understanding of how aesthetic judgements are formed and function. In order to examine how critical and popular assumptions surrounding popular films affect the pedagogy and theory of popular culture study, this essay will discuss two films with very different histories of production and reception: Jean Renoir's classic plea for pacifism, La Grande Illusion (France, 1937) and Sylvester Stallone's recent New Cold War box office hit, Rocky IV (USA, 1985). I have chosen these particular films because, as I will argue, they are similar in many

136

ways, yet *La Grande Illusion* is usually considered "high art" and thus revered, while any Rocky film is usually considered popular culture, and thus reviled.[2]

On what are such aesthetic distinctions based? And how do we decide what constitutes "high" and what constitutes "popular" culture as regards to *film*, a collectively produced, technologically complex, widely marketed art form? In a second part of this paper I will look at how critical discourses—ranging from traditional approaches to the study of literature and art, to the Frankfurt School, to Althusser, to postmodernism, to British cultural studies—answer these questions, and explore what their answers may mean for the cross-cultural study of films like *Rocky IV* and *La Grande Illusion*.

Finally, I will draw on my experiences teaching film, critical theory and popular culture at the University of North Carolina-Chapel Hill to suggest how student reactions (in Tony Bennett's words, "popular readings"[3]) may be used to challenge and extend theoretical models, and vice versa. As promoter and referee of the match between *Rocky IV* and *La Grande Illusion*, I am thus also intentionally pitting "lightweights" (students) against "heavyweights" (theorists). By so doing, I hope to demonstrate the advantages which emerge from not only juxtaposing but also connecting theory and pedagogy, high or elite art and popular culture.

I.

At first sight *Rocky IV* and *La Grande Illusion* seem to offer few points of comparison. They were made in different countries, in different eras, under different political regimes, and with access to very different technologies. Renoir's socialist sympathies are completely at odds with Stallone's tributes to Reagan.[4] The French Popular Front of the mid 30s is a far cry from the Reagan government of the late 80s. And needless to say, the two films were promoted and distributed in very different ways: to take just one example, though advertising gimmicks like dolls constitute profitable subsidiary marketing strategies for Stallone's movies, especially the Rambo series, there were no Jean Gabin dolls, despite his appearance in several of Renoir's films.[5]

Popular journalism and academic criticism alike treat the two films very differently. *La Grande Illusion* is praised as high art while *Rocky IV* is dismissed as "mere" popular culture. Scores of academic books and articles have been written on Renoir and *La Grande Illusion*. The film is universally regarded as a classic, beloved and acclaimed by both the right and the left, hailed as non-ideological because it promotes peace and brotherhood. It is often cited as one of the top ten films of all time, and Renoir is lauded as one of the greatest directors.[6] The tendency of French critics, especially, to describe films as products of individual "auteurs" contributes to the downplaying of the collaborative efforts behind this particular film. At the same time it obscures recognition of film in general as an industrialized production.[7]

Rocky IV, on the other hand, has, with few exceptions, been categorized as manipulative, formulaic, war-mongering trash.[8] Newsweek summarizes mainstream critical reactions to the film as follows: "the daily reviewers called it empty, crude, primitive, boring, bloated, hollow, mush-headed, butter-brained, elephantine, witless, redundant and, in one Hobbesian spasm in The Baltimore Sun, 'loud, stupid, nasty, brutish and short.' "[9] Although much has been written about Stallone, almost all of it has been in magazines and newspapers like People or The National Enquirer.[10] No doubt Rocky IV's position as the fourth, though by no means the final, sequel in the Rocky series fuels critical and popular perceptions of it as an industry product and nothing more.

Despite all these differences, however, Rocky IV and La Grande Illusion are in many ways alike. Both were made as anti-war films, and weave entertainment and politics into the stories they tell. By merging the fictional creations Maréchal and Rocky with the star images of Jean Gabin and Sylvester Stallone, both create characters who are at once sex symbols, men's men, working class heroes and national monuments.[11] Finally, both make overt, though contrasting statements about nationality and class, individualism and collectivity, gender and sexuality, and even war and peace.

Two key sequences in particular offer multiple points of comparison. The first is the French and English prisoners' Christmas pageant, midway through La Grande Illusion, where they amicably perform "Marguerite" and "It's a Long Way to Tipperary" but conclude by defiantly singing the "Marseillaise." The second is Rocky's fight against and victory over the Russian boxer, Ivan Drago, which culminates in his adulation by the Russian people and the Politburo at the end of Rocky IV.

Among the similarities between these sequences are the following: both involve stage events; both are performed before an audience; both rely on the myth of Christmas as a time of peace, good will and brotherhood to bridge and/or disguise adversarial relations between nations; both invoke and rewrite the past to suit the needs of the present; and both ally the film spectator in the theater with the audiences in the films through the skillful editing of sounds and images. Thanks to the diverse messages which emerge from the blending of fiction, fact and fantasy, young and old, black and white, women and men, we all sing along with Maréchal and root for Rocky.[12]

There are, of course, differences between the two sequences. In the case of La Grande Illusion, the inclusion of a play within the film provides a break in the basic narrative line: for a moment, Maréchal and his companions forget they are prisoners of war trying to escape from German camps. Furthermore, in *La Grande Illusion* there is a more overt play with sexuality and gender, a more conscious confusion of "reality" and "illusion," and a decided preference for collectivity over individualism. The English (though not the French) soldiers dress as women; dolly shots and pans repeatedly flout the 180 degree rule of classic Hollywood film, shifting from the audience's to the performers' points of view within a single shot and thereby uniting the actors with their audience and vice versa; and, while the final shot begins with the hero, Maréchal, in the foreground in close-up, it ends on all the prisoners in long shot. In this sequence, nationality thus seems more important than class, whereas in the film as a whole language and dialects, shot size, framing and props distinguish and group characters according to social and class background far more than according to nationality.

In contrast, Rocky's fight is the climax of *Rocky IV* and the apogee of the New Cold War rhetoric which underpins it. Class is merged with, even submerged in, nationality, and unity, if not collectivity, is achieved through identification with the individual as hero. The limited dialogue and the insistence on spectacle throughout *Rocky IV* continue on a global scale the work of nation building and unification begun by the first Hollywood films: unlike *La Grande Illusion*, with *Rocky IV* there is virtually no need for sub-titles to convey the film's message to a foreign audience.[13] In this sequence and even more in the film as a whole, reality and illusion are more fused than confused: there are constant references to other media and earlier Rocky films, and frequent appearances by real-life sports commentators and entertainment figures like Warner Wolf and James Brown. The only masquerade is male, and muscular: Stallone's muscles function as costume, clothing and disguising him as a man, and compensating for the fear of weakness and aging which haunts the first half of the films.[14] The insistence on muscular masculinity is reinforced by rapid editing, innumerable close-ups, constantly shifting camera positions and a blaring sound track.[15]

Although there is no denying the significance of these differences, what is equally of interest is the repetition of categories and contradictions in two films made half a century apart. For both sequences foreground representation and reality at the same time as they hide technology behind narrative. In both politics and entertainment peacefully coexist: everyone, even the aristocrats, the bureaucrats, the "enemy," has a good time, yet the stocky, macho, working-class hero nonetheless triumphs.

Why, then, if there are so many points of similarity in the two films' inscription of sexuality, gender, class and nationality is one denigrated by critics, condemned as popular culture, while the other is applauded, elevated to high art? After all, *both* films have been and are *popular*. Christopher Faulkner describes *La Grande Illusion* as originally a commercial venture: "[The film] was handsomely produced by Réalisation d'Art Cinématographic fully expecting a profitable return.... By all accounts, its premiere on 4 June 1937 at the Marivaux Cinema, Paris, and subsequent exhibition history in London and New York did not disappoint the producers."[16] According to *Newsweek*, *Rocky IV* grossed $32 million in five days, "the strongest nonsummer opening ever,...push[ing] the total domestic take for the [Rocky] series over $400 million."[17]

Given the financial success and popular appeal of both *La Grande Illusion* and *Rocky IV*, as well as their many other points of similarity, it seems appropriate to return now to my original questions: how are we to distinguish popular culture from high or elite culture with regard to mass media and film texts? Are such distinctions necessarily worth making? What do they mean for pedagogy and theory?

II

Over the years a variety of theoretical responses to these questions have been proposed. Many literary and film theorists continue to disdain mass and popular culture as purely ideological and avoid dealing with them by positioning them outside the realm of "Literature" or "Art," defined as the only valid objects of study and abstracted from social networks. Questions of class and the politics of production, exhibition and distribution are thereby side-stepped. As Edward Said points out, the idea that art exists for art's sake is exacerbated by the ever increasing specialization and fragmentation of academic disciplines.[18] Within this critical framework *Rocky IV* would never be considered worthy of attention while *La Grande Illusion* would be abstracted from the social conditions of its filming and viewing and held up to audiences for veneration as "great art," a film "classic."

In contrast to the total dismissal of popular culture as a theoretical object, Marxist critics like Benjamin, Horkheimer, Adorno and Althusser acknowledge the existence and importance of mass and popular culture and integrate historical, cultural and ideological analysis. But ultimately, they, too, perpetuate the value-laden separation of art from mass media and popular culture.[19] With the exception of Benjamin, Frankfurt School theorists view mass culture as manipulative of the masses, although they critique bourgeois art as elitist.[20] For Horkheimer and Adorno, the categories "high art" and "style" remain at least partially operative, though they are now rephrased as "autonomous art" and "technique," and conceived of in dialectical relationship to mass culture.[21] Film is equated with ideology and excluded from the realm of autonomous art for two reasons: 1) in it the means of reproduction—technology—is more important than aesthetic technique, and 2) technology is controlled by the culture industry.[22]

For the Frankfurt School, *Rocky IV* would provide an easy target: its plot is so blatantly ideological, and its marketing as a sequel and a star vehicle is so clearly profit-oriented. *La Grande Illusion*, on the other hand, might be more favorably viewed, thanks to Renoir's anti-Fascist politics and his support of the Popular Front. In either case, however, emphasis would be placed on production at the expense of reception, for, again with the exception of Benjamin, a deep-seated distrust of cinema audiences permeates Frankfurt School theory. The film spectator is seen as a passive consumer of illusions set in place by the seeming objectivity of the photographic image: "sustained thought is out of the question if the spectator is not to miss the relentless rush of facts."[23] What the spectator likes is beside the point, for entertainment is escapism and "amusement always reveals the influence of business.... Pleasure always means not to think about anything, to forget suffering even where it is shown. Basically it is helplessness. It is flight; not, as is asserted, flight from a wretched reality, but from the last remaining thought of resistance."[24] In this scenario, anyone who cheers Rocky or even Maréchal on to victory thus blocks or denies the reality of her or his own historical situation, at the same time as s/he gives all responsibility for action over to a fictional character.

Like Horkheimer and Adorno, Althusser also distinguishes between high culture and mass media in his discussions of art and ideology. In Althusser's model art and ideology are tightly linked, but not identical. Ideology is equivalent to lived experience. It "has very little to do with consciousness.... It is profoundly unconscious."[25] Where the appreciation of cultural works is concerned, ideology thus seems to characterize what Bourdieu calls "popular taste" as opposed to "intellectual" or "educated taste": "popular taste" affirms a continuity between art and life.[26] For Althusser "real art" ultimately stands in opposition to "ideology" because it calls attention to ideology through formal distancing devices. In terms reminiscent of the Russian Formalists, Althusser writes: "the specific function of the work of art is to make *visible*, by establishing a distance from it, the reality of the existing ideology."[27]

But the examples Althusser gives of "real art" (Balzac, Tolstoy, Solzhenitsyn and the expressionist painter Cremonini), nowhere include references to mass media.[28] Instead, the press, radio and television, and, one would imagine, film, are described as part of what Althusser calls the "communications ideological state apparatus" (ISA), which is separate from the cultural ISA (comprised of Literature, the Arts and sport), even though both ISAs function to establish and maintain state power without recourse to repression.[29]

The distinction Althusser makes between the communications and cultural ISAs is confusing, however: where do popular films like *Rocky IV* fit in this model? Are they still to be opposed to "Art" films like *La Grande Illusion*? The situation is further complicated because technology is not addressed per se in Althusser's writings on art and ideology, though science is opposed to art: science enables us to 'know' ideology while art helps us to 'perceive,' 'feel,' and 'see' ideology.[30] One strongly suspects Althusser, like Horkheimer and Adorno, would despise *Rocky IV*, though he might possibly be prepared to grant *La Grande Illusion* the title of "Art." In any event, because in his discussion of mass media he ignores technology and fails to acknowledge the class, social and educational factors which shape his own aesthetic and political judgments, he unwittingly perpetuates a traditionally upper class French fondness for aristocratic culture and loses sight of the historical and class dimensions of aesthetic perceptions.[31]

Postmodern theory offers yet another pairing of elite and popular culture which ends in divorce. Like Althusser and the Frankfurt School, Baudrillard and other postmodern theorists situate and discuss cultural texts and their production and reception within a historical framework. But unlike Marxist analyses, too often this framework is conceptualized in terms of oppositions between artistic periods and technological developments and not as an ongoing dialectic between cultural super-structure and economic infrastructure. Thus postmodern theory describes postmodern art as a reaction to and rupture in modernist aesthetics, despite the fact that postmodern art often incorporates and extends modernist strategies in its playful mixtures of high art, mass media and everyday life. Just how to define postmodernism and modernism is, obviously, in question, not least because the term "postmodern" is now applied to everything from the arts to theory to emotions to economics.[32]

Furthermore, while there is no doubt that postmodern theory is more open to popular culture and more attentive to consumption than either the Frankfurt School or Althusser, nostalgia for the past still coexists with enthusiasm for the present. Nowhere is this more apparent than in postmodern analyses of film. In an article entitled "Postmodernism or The Cultural Logic of Late Capitalism," Jameson clearly prefers the stars and the genre and auteur films of the 30s and 40s to contemporary actors and films. In this context *Rocky IV* would again be an object of derision, despite its characteristically postmodern incorporation of real life figures like Warner Wolf and James Brown into the film fiction and its mixture of music video and realist film. Moreover, repeated *National Enquirer* testimonials notwithstanding, Sylvester Stallone is not (or not yet!) a star or personality of the status of Marlon Brando, Laurence Olivier or Clark Gable—actors Jameson mentions in his discussion of what he calls the " 'death of the subject' in the institution of the star"—whereas Jean Gabin might easily be included.[33] Ironically, for postmodern analyses of film, the very culture industry of the 1930s which Horkheimer and Adorno so abhorred now seems not such a bad thing at all: even Hollywood genre or series films made around the same time as *La Grande Illusion* (the *Thin Man* or *Gold-Diggers* movies, for example) are now considered classics.

The pessimism and mistrust of technology and audiences which permeated Horkheimer and Adorno's discussions of the culture industry also linger on in postmodern analyses of mass media. Baudrillard is every bit as scornful of mass media audiences as Horkheimer and Adorno were. Symptomatic is his argument that meaning and the real have imploded under the sheer weight of media discourses which "subjugate the masses to meaning."[34] That there might be different ways today to watch *Rocky IV* or *La Grande Illusion* is out of the question. The very finality and generality of Baudrillard's statements betray the arrogance of the white European male. After all, feminists have insisted for nearly twenty years that there is no *one* meaning, and that the very notion of *one* meaning excludes women, blacks, gays, workers and others.[35] And as Stuart Hall scathingly recalls: "Three-quarters of the human race have not yet entered what we are pleased to call 'the real.' "[36] Baudrillard's argument needs rephrasing: the question is not *whether* meaning has imploded but *whose* meaning has imploded.

Viewed from this angle, the ubiquitousness of postmodern culture and the implosion of meaning are not necessarily negative, any more than high art is necessarily "better" than popular culture.[37] This, indeed, is the perspective adopted by Hall, Bennett and other British theorists. They maintain that there are no "good" or "bad" objects of study. Similarly, neither technology nor entertainment is a priori good or bad. What counts is how audiences interact with and *use* cultural texts in specific historical contexts. For once the fact that *Rocky IV* and *La Grande Illusion* appeal to audiences thus becomes an incentive to study and even compare them in order to ascertain why, when and where they are popular. For British cultural studies theorists, aesthetic and ideological value judgments are not inherent in texts. As a result there is, in Lawrence Grossberg's words: "no necessary correspondence between a text and its politics."[38] Textual politics change and can be changed. Because politics, not aesthetics, are key, British theorists regard themselves not just as theorists, but also as political activists.[39] Crucially, British cultural studies do not argue for aesthetic relativism: *Rocky IV* and *La Grande Illusion* are not equivalently "good," rather they can be read as similar, given specific political needs at a particular moment in time.[40]

Nevertheless, no form of cultural theory adequately addresses the dilemmas students and teachers encounter when analyzing mass media and film texts. With the exception of British cultural theory, all the approaches I have summarized above—the continuation of "art for art's sake," Frankfurt School theory, Althusser and postmodernism—not only separate popular and high culture, but also divorce theory from pedagogy, and intellectuals from everyone else. How to bridge all these gaps?

III

Let me return to my original examples of *La Grande Illusion* and *Rocky IV* and incorporate pedagogy with theory. In general, the students I worked with at the University of North Carolina preferred *Rocky IV* to *La Grande Illusion*, although some would always opt for European "art" films over Hollywood blockbusters. John Waters' sarcastic yet sincere description of his own fondness for the European avant-garde sums up the latter attitude nicely: "Give me black and white, subtitles, and a tiny budget and I'm impressed...."[41]

The reasons most students gave for their preference for *Rocky IV* implicitly challenge certain cherished tenets of critical theory. For students, even more than for theorists, *all* film is equated with entertainment, regarded as separate not only from art but also from ideology. Film value is defined according to whether the film is considered to be "realistic," a term usually used with reference to their own life experiences. *La Grande Illusion* is "unrealistic" in their eyes because, to take just one example, people today do not dress or act like von Stroheim, de Boeldieu or even Maréchal. "Realism" is also, however, equated with technological progress. Color is thus "better" than black and white, rapid montage "better" than long takes, elaborate sound mixes "better" than simpler sound tracks, and, for American students, English-language films are of course "better" than foreign-language films.

These preferences challenge Althusserian divisions between art, ideology and science, at the same time as they point up the elitist refusal to account for pleasure and the mistrust of technology which subtends, though differently, Frankfurt School and postmodern theory. Furthermore, they contradict the isolationism of "art for art's sake" by positing "realism" and experience as prerequisites of aesthetic value. Nonetheless, in seeming contradiction, since all film is supposedly regarded as pure entertainment, *La Grande Illusion* will, according to these criteria, more easily be recognized as a film classic, bordering on high art ("it's a great film for its time," in the words of one of my students), *because* it seems less realistic, less technologically sophisticated. The reluctance of British cultural studies to differentiate between popular culture and high or elite culture is validated here, though in a rather curious way: student assessments of films include aesthetic value judgments as much as critical assessments do, and even show an awareness of historical shifts in cultural texts, although these shifts are primarily categorized as technological "progress."

Student reactions to *Rocky IV* and *La Grande Illusion* thus highlight the problems facing comparative popular culture study, and, when put on an equal footing with critical reactions, expose the extent to which ideas about technology, entertainment, ideology and commerce color both popular and intellectual aesthetic value judgments.

IV

But who wins when *Rocky IV* meets *La Grande Illusion?* What political resonances emerge from comparisons of American and European popular films? I find that the juxtaposition of films like these draws several adversaries together—popular and high culture, pedagogy and theory, students and teachers—with the following results.

First, the fact that *Rocky IV* and *La Grande Illusion* have so much in common for all their many differences demonstrates the tenuousness, if not the futility, of hard and fast distinctions between popular and elite culture. Comparisons between the two, or between equivalent films, can be used to explore the bases for their political and aesthetic differences, as well as to chart the ways in which today's blockbusters, unlike 30s films, address and construct the world as a global village, even though the lack of cinemas and TV sets in Third World countries means this universalizing strategy is, at best, a fantasy.[42] Yet—and this is crucial—the similarities between *Rocky IV* and *La Grande Illusion* can only be perceived and appreciated if we compare their use of technology, reliance on stars, work with narrative and so forth *without* initially concentrating on their aesthetic value. Only in this way will we be able to describe not only the shifts but also the continuities in cinematic representations of sexuality, gender, class and nationality.

Second, the ways student evaluations echo, contradict and transform theoretical categories used to judge mass media texts may encourage reexaminations of these categories. Hopefully, such reexaminations will result in more accurate assessments, by both students and theorists, of the merits and drawbacks implicit in the choice of one formulation over another, as well as demonstrate that canons are formed, not fixed, and that while aesthetic evaluation exists, it changes.

Last but not least, comparisons of films like *Rocky IV* and *La Grande Illusion* offer teachers the chance to introduce and critique critical theories of mass media and popular culture without excluding or denigrating student reactions. On the contrary, teachers learn to acknowledge that, to quote Tony Bennett: " 'Untutored' [or popular] readings are just as real and material in their effects as 'tutored' ones and may, indeed, be considerably more influential."[43] By studying so-called "high art" and popular culture at the same time, student interest and, I would stress, *proficiency* in reading mass media texts is recognized and utilized. The hierarchical relationship between teachers and students is in part undermined, and some of the gaps between teachers as experts and students as apprentices are bridged. Together the two groups might even, as Angela McRobbie suggests, "provide a basis for the production of new meanings, new cultural expressions...."[44]

Knowledge, after all, is a process, not a product.[45] It may be that *everyone* wins when *Rocky IV* meets *La Grande Illusion*—students and teachers, pedagogy and theory, "popular culture" and "high art"—and *everyone* changes. But Rocky says it so well it seems only fair to let him have the last word:

Thank you. I came here tonight and I didn't know what to expect. I seen a lot of people hatin' me and I didn't know what to feel about that so I guess I didn't like you much none either. During this fight I seen a lot of changin'. The way yous felt about me and the way I felt about you. In here there were two guys killin' each other, but I guess that's better than 20 million. What I'm tryin' to say is, that if I can change and you can change, everybody can change!

Notes

I wish to thank my students at the University of North Carolina, Chapel Hill, without whom this paper would not have been conceived. Thanks also to Gina Marchetti, Scot Nygren and Eric Arnould for many stimulating discussions on the issues raised here.

[1]Pierre Bourdieu, *Distinction: A Social Critique of the Judgement of Taste*, trans. Richard Nice (Cambridge: Harvard University Press, 1984) xi.

[2]The term "popular culture" is difficult to define. In addition to the idea that popular culture is what is "well-liked by many people," a definition which, as Tony Bennett notes, "permits of hardly any exclusions," there are at least three other uses of the term: 1) "popular culture" is what is left-over from high culture; 2) "popular culture" is synonymous with mass culture; and 3) "popular culture" is equal to folk or working class culture. See Tony Bennett, "Popular Culture: A 'Teaching Object,' " *Screen Education* 34 (Spring 1980): 20:21. See, further, Colin MacCabe for a critique of Bennett's analysis. Colin MacCabe, "Defining Popular Culture," *High Theory, Low Culture*, ed. Colin MacCabe (New York: St. Martin's Press, 1986) 1-10.

[3]Bennett defines "popular readings" as "readings produced outside the academy, at a considerable remove from, and relatively untouched by, the discourses of textual criticism that circulate within it." He uses this term rather than the term "untutored readings" because the former "implies readings that may be assessed as valid and productive on their own terms" whereas the latter "implies an absence or a lack...; readings that 'don't count' and whose only destiny, unless they are ear-marked for preservation as curiosities, is to be 'corrected.' " Tony Bennett, "Texts, Readers, Reading Formations," *Bulletin of the Midwest Modern Language Association* (Spring 1983): 3-4.

In what follows I will consciously retain the multiple meanings of both "popular culture" and "high art" in order to trace the intersections, overlaps, divergences and contradictions between and among theoretical discourses and popular readings.

[4]The political allegiances of the directors have been recognized in the official reception given their films: *La Grande Illusion* was banned in Nazi Germany (Goebbels termed it "cinematographic enemy number one"), in Italy (Mussolini called it "anti-heroic") and in Vichy France (it was labelled "demoralizing"), but it was promoted by Roosevelt ("All the democracies of the world must see this film"). Reagan loves Rambo and has incorporated him (as earlier Dirty Harry) into his own rhetorical right-wing world ("In the spirit of Rambo, let me tell you we're going to win this time"). In *Cobra* (1986), Stallone returned the compliment, prominently displaying a portrait of Reagan on the wall of Cobretti's office.

[5]As Armand Mattelart, Xavier Delcourt and Michelle Mattelart point out, astronomical increases in film production costs have been accompanied by new means of distribution and promotion as well as by new methods of financing. Today's popular Hollywood films often participate in a "commodity circuit" where "a film company can expect between 6 and 10% of the retail price of each by-product." Armand Mattelart, Xavier Delcourt and Michelle Mattelart, *International Image Markets*, trans. David Buxton (London: Comedia Publishing Group, 1984) 79.

[6]Christopher Faulkner argues, correctly I think, that the majority of critical readings of *La Grande Illusion* are misreadings: "*La Grande Illusion* tends to be the most widely admired of Renoir's films (the fifth greatest film of all time according to an international jury of 117 critics at the Brussels World's Fair in 1958), but I cannot help thinking that this admiration does the film an injustice, or rather, depends upon a misreading. This film, perhaps more than any other directed by Renoir during the thirties, is subject to that commonplace liability of auteurism that reads the man through the work (or the work in the man). By universalizing the work and essentializing the man the conclusion has been reached that Renoir does not take sides, that in his all-embracing humanity he rises above politics." Christopher Faulkner, *The Social Cinema of Jean Renoir* (Princeton University Press: Princeton, 1986) 85.

[7]See Eugène Lourié, "Grand Illusions," *American Film* 10:1 (Jan.-Feb. 1985): 29-34, for a description of the filming of *La Grande Illusion*. Lourié was the set designer for the film.

Mattelart, Delcourt and Mattelart note that the French tend to separate the 'cultural' from the 'technical,' and to divorce culture from the historical conditions of its production. See Mattelart 15.

[8]Tom O'Brien's review of *Rocky IV* is the only positive one I have found. He describes the film as an intellectual masterpiece, directed by a new cinematic auteur. "Perhaps it is a tribute to Stallone's dazzling subtlety that so many viewers have not realized that *Rocky IV* is actually a shrewd satire on the sources of misunderstanding in world affairs," he says. Tom O'Brien, *Commonweal* 113.1 (January 17, 1986): 16-17. Examples of negative reviews are: Peter Goldman, "Rocky and Rambo," *Newsweek* 106.26 (December 23, 1985): 58-62; Jack Kroll, "Socking It to the Russians," *Newsweek* 106.24 (December 9, 1985): 92; and Richard Schickel, "Win the Battle, Lose the War," *Time* 126.23 (December 9, 1985): 110.

[9]Goldman 58.

[10]There are, however, a few exceptions. See, for example, Steven D. Stark, "Ten Years into the Stallone Era: What It, Uh, All Means," *New York Times* (February 22, 1987): H19-20. Stark interviews a number of film scholars who comment, most often sympathetically, on Stallone's popularity.

[11]Gabin was cast as a working class hero and sex symbol in a number of 1930s films: Renoir's *Les Bas-Fonds* (1936) and *La Bête humaine* (1938), Duvivier's *La Belle équipe* (1936) and *Pepe le Moko* (1937), Carné's *Quai des brumes* (1938) and *Le Jour se lève* (1939) and Grémillon's *Gueule d'amour* (1937) and *Remorques* (1940). Stallone's roles as Rocky, Rambo and Cobra also combine class, sexuality and

nationality. The films both actors have made utilize them as stars, as types and as actors, merging their extra—and inter-textual reputations with their performances. In *La Grande Illusion* and *Rocky IV*, even Gabin's and Stallone's gestures, dialects and vocabularies establish them as tough yet tender guys. Only the Frenchman's volubility and the American's stalwart silence set them apart. See Richard Dyer, *Stars* (London: British Film Institute, 1979), for a comprehensive discussion of the functioning of stars in Hollywood and European film.

[12]The audience for the Rocky films testify to Stallone's capacity to unite and please a crowd: "nearly half the cash customers...are over 25, and nearly half are women." Goldman 58.

[13]As Mattelart, Delcourt and Mattelart point out, the French firm Gaumont has now adopted the same strategy of universality, making films with little dialogue, "superstars and spectacular, often violent images which have no need for subtitles." Mattelart 99.

[14]See Christine Holmlund, "Sequels and Remakes in Politics and Film: *Down and Out in Beverly Hills, Rocky IV, Aliens* and the New Cold War," forthcoming in *Jump Cut*, for a more detailed analysis of the fears of weakness and the fantasies of strength which are inscribed, created and undercut in contemporary Hollywood New Cold War films.

[15]Within patriarchal societies, the status of the male body is far more precarious than that of the female body, because the threat of castration lurks everywhere. Semi-naked, ultra-muscular male bodies—Stallone's stock in trade—seem natural, the epitome of the equation of biology, sexuality and gender on which patriarchal power is based. In reality, however, they are the products of work in a gym, unnatural, and even threatening because they are so exaggerated. Thus, as I have argued elsewhere, "[body builder] Lou Ferrigno's...casting as the Hulk and Arnold Schwarzenegger's success as Conan the Barbarian and the Terminator are not coincidental. Their excessive muscularity has made them oddities and has only increased male anxiety that, to quote Richard Dyer...'the penis is not a patch on the phallus.'" Christine Holmlund, "Visible Difference and Flex Appeal: The Body, Race, Sex and Sexuality in the *Pumping Iron* Films," *Cinema Journal* 28.4 (Summer 1989): 38-51. See also Richard Dyer, "Don't Look Now," *Screen* 23.3-4 (Sept.-Oct. 1982): 67-68.

[16]Faulkner 85. Gérard Talon's study of Popular Front films corroborates this view. According to Talon, Renoir's sensitivity to public taste in 1930s France is manifest in his choice of setting, time period and genre. Faulkner cites Talon in support of his own argument: "between 1936 and 1938 a love story had a 63% chance of interesting the public if it took place during the First World War, in a military setting, and raised problems concerning national duty." Faulkner 89. See Gérard Talon, "Le Cinéma du Front Populaire," *Cinéma 75*, 194 (January 1975): 34-36.

[17]Goldman 58. Goldman also offers statistics on *Rambo*'s box office success: "$32 million in ticket sales during its first six days, the third best launch in history." Ibid. *Rocky* grossed $88.5 million, *Rocky II* $58.5 million and *Rocky III* $101.3 million. Compare these figures with those for three other series: *Star Wars*, $255.4 million, *The Empire Strikes Back* $163.5 million, *Return of the Jedi* $214.3 million; *Jaws* $135.5 million, *Jaws II* $60 million, *Jaws 3-D* $36.4 million; and *Superman* $193 million, *Superman II* $90 million, *Superman III* $52.7 million. See Kroll 92 for more.

[18]Said offers a biting analysis of the current situation. He writes: "[T]he prevailing mode of intellectual discourse is militantly antimethodological, if by methodological we mean a questioning of the structure of fields and discourses themselves. A principle of silent exclusion operates within and at the boundaries of discourse; this has now become so internalized that fields, disciplines and their discourses have taken on the status of immutable durability....To acquire a position of authority within the field is...to be involved internally in the formation of a canon, which usually turns

out to be a blocking device for methodological and disciplinary self-questioning." Edward W. Said, "Opponents, Audiences, Constituencies and Community," *The Anti-Aesthetic*, ed. Hal Foster (Port Townsend: Bay Press, 1983) 149.

[19]Bennett argues that Marxist theorists have only taken over and continued bourgeois aesthetic categories in their examination of literature. "Marxist criticism has, for the greater part of its history, been an essentially bourgeois enterprise at the level of its founding theoretical assumptions." Tony Bennett, "Marxism and Popular Fiction," *Literature & History* 7.2 (1981): 139.

[20]Benjamin rejoices at the emergence of mass art and the destruction of the aura of bourgeois art, because, as he says: "the total function of art is reversed. Instead of being based on ritual, it begins to be based on another practice—politics." Walter Benjamin, "The Work of Art in the Age of Mechanical Reproduction," *Illuminations* (New York: Schocken, 1969) 224. Adorno finds Benjamin's faith in mechanical reproduction to be overly optimistic. See Theodor Adorno, "Letter to Walter Benjamin of March 18, 1936," *Aesthetics and Politics*, ed. Ronald Taylor (London: Verso, 1977) 120-126. Nevertheless, like Benjamin, he and Horkheimer are vehemently opposed to bourgeois art: "The purity of bourgeois art, which hypostasized itself as a world of freedom in contrast to what was happening in the material world, was from the beginning bought with the exclusion of the lower classes.... Serious art has been withheld from those for whom the hardship and oppression of life make a mockery of seriousness." Max Horkheimer and Theodor Adorno, "The Culture Industry: Enlightenment as Mass Deception," *Dialectic of Enlightenment* (New York: Seabury Press, 1972) 135.

[21]Andreas Huyssen argues that for Adorno, "autonomy was a relational phenomenon....[He] never saw modernism as anything other than a reaction formation to mass culture and commodification, a reaction formation which operated on the level of form and artistic material." Andreas Huyssen, "Mass Culture as Woman," *Studies in Entertainment*, ed. Tania Modleski (Bloomington: Indiana Univ. Press, 1986) 201. Adorno himself writes: "Both [modern art and mass culture] bear the scars of capitalism, both contain elements of change. Both are torn halves of freedom to which, however, they do not add up." Adorno, "Letter to Benjamin" 123. Nonetheless, as many critics have noted, for Horkheimer and Adorno modern art usually adds up to more than mass culture does. See, for example, Fredric Jameson, "Reification and Utopia in Mass Culture," *Social Text* 1.1 (Winter 1979): 132-135.

[22]In contrast once again to Horkheimer and Adorno, Benjamin welcomes technology because it makes art available to a greater number of people and enriches perception. He does, however, acknowledge that: "In Western Europe the capitalistic exploitation of the film denies consideration to modern man's legitimate claim to being reproduced...through illusion-promoting spectacles and dubious speculations." Benjamin 232. Adorno charges that in his enthusiasm Benjamin conflates technique and technology, and thereby collapses crucial distinctions between what he calls the autonomous work of art (modernist art) and bourgeois art. Adorno, "Letter to Benjamin," 121-124.

[23]Horkeimer and Adorno 127.

[24]Horkeimer and Adorno 144. Benjamin, on the other hand, insists that audiences are capable of both critical thought and emotion when watching film, and attributes this capacity once again to technology: "Mechanical reproduction of art changes the reaction of the masses toward art. The reactionary attitude toward a Picasso painting changes into the progressive reaction toward a Chaplin movie. The progressive reaction is characterized by the direct, intimate fusion of visual and emotional enjoyment with the orientation of the expert." Benjamin 234. Adorno labels this confidence "romanticization" and charges that "the laughter of the audience at a cinema...is full of the worst bourgeois sadism." Adorno 123. In "Transparencies on Film,"

however, Adorno's attitudes toward cinema change and draw closer to Benjamin's formulations. Here Adorno pays more attention to changes in film style and cinematic specificity. He also admits that a variety of receptions and uses of film are possible. See Theodor Adorno, "Transparencies on Film," *New German Critique* 24-25 (Fall/Winter 1981-82), 199-203.

For helpful comparisons of Benjamin, Horkheimer and Adorno see Diane Waldman, "Critical Theory and Film: Adorno and 'The Culture Industry' Revisited," *New German Critique* 12 (1977): 39-60 and Miriam Hansen, "Introduction to Adorno," "Transparencies on Film," *New German Critique* 24-25 (Fall/Winter 81-82): 186-198.

[25]Louis Althusser, "Marxism and Humanism," *For Marx* (London: Allen Lane, 1969) 233.

[26]Bourdieu 4.

[27]Louis Althusser, "Cremonini, Painter of the Abstract," *Lenin and Philosophy* (New York: Monthly Review Press, 1971) 241-242. Shklovsky's concept of "defamiliarization" is comparable in many ways: "[A]rt exists...to make one feel things, to make the stone *stony*. The purpose of art is to impart the sensation of things as they are perceived and not as they are known. The technique of art is to make objects 'unfamiliar,' to make forms difficult, to increase the difficulty and length of perception because the process of perception is an aesthetic end in itself and must be prolonged." Victor Shklovsky, "Art as Technique," *Russian Formalist Criticism*, ed. Lee T. Lemon and Marion J. Reis (Lincoln: University of Nebraska Press, 1965) 12.

[28]See Althusser, "A Letter on Art in Reply to André Daspre," *Lenin and Philosophy* 221-227, and "Cremonini, Painter of the Abstract," *Lenin and Philosophy* 229-242 for discussions of the relationships between art and ideology.

[29]Althusser, "Ideology and Ideological State Apparatuses," *Lenin and Philosophy* 143.

[30]Althusser, "A Letter on Art" 223.

[31]Bourdieu argues that left-and right-wing intellectuals alike indulge in "self-interested representations of culture" by failing to acknowledge their own points of view in the "games of culture." As a result, their supposedly objective analyses of other points of view are really incomplete and reductive objectifications of the range of possible positions. Bourdieu 12-13.

[32]As Dick Hebdige notes: "To say 'post' is to say 'past'—...questions of periodization are inevitably raised. There is however little agreement as to what it is we are alleged to have surpassed, when that passage is supposed to have occurred and what effects it is supposed to have had." Dick Hebdige, "Postmodernism and 'The Other Side,' " *Journal of Communication Inquiry* 10.2 (Summer 1986): 79. Jameson, too, speaks of the difficulty of periodization and definition, but then goes on to write about everything under the sun. He says that postmodernism should be considered "a cultural dominant," not a style, in order to allow for "the presence and coexistence of a range of very different, yet subordinate features." Fredric Jameson, "Post-modernism, or The Cultural Logic of Late Capitalism," *New Left Review* 146 (July-August): 56. In contrast to Jameson's eclectic approach, Baudrillard takes television and advertising as the prime examples and models of postmodernism: "Television is the ultimate and perfect object of this new era" and "advertising invades everything." Jean Baudrillard, "The Ecstasy of Communication," *The Anti-Aesthetic* 127 and 129.

[33]Jameson writes: "The immediately preceding generation projected its various roles through, and by way of, well-known 'off-screen' personalities, who often connoted rebellion and non-conformism. The latest generation of starring actors continues to assure the conventional functions of stardom (most notably, sexuality) but in the

utter absence of 'personality' in the older sense...." Fredric Jameson, "Postmodernism, or The Cultural Logic of Late Capitalism" 68. For a similar appraisal of post-modern films in relation to so-called classic Hollywood film, see also Andrew Britton, "Blissing Out: The Politics of Reaganite Entertainment," *Movie* 31-32 (Winter 1986): 1-42.

[34]Jean Baudrillard, "The Implosion of Meaning in the Media and the Information of the Social in the Masses," *Myth of Information: Technology and Post-Industrial Culture*, ed. Kathleen Woodward (Madison: Coda Press, 1980) 142.

[35]Increasingly feminists critique postmodern theory along these lines. See, for example, Barbara Creed, "From Here to Modernity—Feminism and Postmodernism," *Screen* 28.2 (Spring 1987): 47-68, Anne Balsamo, "Un-Wrapping the Post-modern: A Feminist Glance," *Journal of Communication Inquiry* 11.1 (Winter 1987): 64-72, and Nancy Miller, "The Text's Heroine: A Feminist Critic and Her Fictions," *Diacritics* 12.2 (Summer 1982): 48-53.

[36]Stuart Hall, "On Postmodernism and Articulation," ed. Lawrence Grossberg, *Journal of Communication Inquiry* 10.2 (Summer 1986): 46.

[37]See Angela McRobbie, "Postmodernism and Popular Culture," *Journal of Communication Inquiry* 10:2 (Summer 1986): 108-116 and Tania Modleski, ed., *Studies in Entertainment* (Bloomington: Indiana University Press, 1986) for more optimistic appraisals of both popular culture and postmodernism.

[38]Lawrence Grossberg, "History, Politics and Postmodernism: Stuart Hall and Cultural Studies," *Journal of Communication Inquiry* 10:2 (Summer 1986): 66. For a more detailed presentation of these ideas see Tony Bennett, "Texts, Readers, Reading Formation" 3-17 and Gillian Swanson, "Rethinking Representation," *Screen* 27.5 (Sept.-Oct. 1986): 26.

[39]Postmodern theory and British cultural studies often overlap. This is not surprising, since they are contemporaneous and draw on much the same intellectual history. At their extremes, however, the two disagree fiercely overpostmodernism and Althusser.

[40]See John Fiske, "British Cultural Studies and Television," *Channels of Discourse*, ed. Robert C. Allen (Chapel Hill: University of North Carolina Press, 1987) 254-288, for a succinct discussion of British cultural studies. Fiske notes that three basic Marxist assumptions underlie cultural studies: 1) "meanings and the making of them...are indivisibly linked to the social structure and can only be explained in terms of that structure and its history"; 2) "capitalist societies are divided societies—[and] social relations are understood in terms of social power, in terms of a structure of domination and subordination that is never static but is always the site of contestation and struggle"; and 3) "culture is ideological." Fiske 254-256.

[41]John Waters, "Guilty Pleasures," *Film Comment* 19.4 (July-August 1983): 20.

[42]Mattelart, Delcourt and Mattelart cite the following 1981-1982 UNESCO statistics as proof that the "global village" is a Western fabrication:

Whereas in Europe, the number of television sets is about 275 per 1,000 inhabitants, this figure drops to 90 per 1,000 in Latin America and 11 per 1,000 in Africa. But even these figures mask extreme variations within Africa and Latin America. Argentina, for example, has 204 sets per 1,000 inhabitants whereas Haiti has only 11. In Africa, the French colony Reunion comes first with 130 sets; at the other extreme, we find the central African Republic with 0.2 sets per 1,000 inhabitants—a grand total of 400 sets in the whole country.... Similar disparities exist with...cinemas (France 5,000; West Africa 300 for 55 million people)....

Mattelart 23-24.

[43]Tony Bennett, "Text and Social Process: The Case of James Bond," *Screen Education* 41 (Winter/Spring 1982): 9.

[44]McRobbie 112.

[45]For other discussions of the links between the pedagogy and theory of popular culture, see, for example, Judith Williamson, "How Does Girl Number Twenty Understand Ideology," *Screen Education* 40 (Autumn-Winter 1981-2): 80-87; David Lusted, "Why Pedagogy?," *Screen* 27.5 (Sept.-Oct. 1986): 2-14; Tony Bennett, "Popular Culture as Teaching Object"; and Ian Connell, "'Progressive' Pedagogy?," *Screen* 24.3 (May-June 1983): 50-54.

Contributors

Chantal Cinquin writes about cultural phenomenons from the perspective of psychoanalysis and semiotics. Her book *Le Refoulé de l'histoire* is a contribution to the theory of representation of the origins of civilization in archeological publications, museology, tourist brochures and literature. She is currently researching the relationship of the visual arts and psychoanalysis in an attempt to develop an approach to psychoanalysis, combining visual arts and the psychoanalytical theory.

Yolanda Broyles González is with the Department of Germanic Language and Literatures and Department of Chicano Studies at University of California Santa Barbara, CA.

Christine Holmlund is Assistant Professor in Romance Languages at the University of Tennessee, teaches courses in French, Film and Women's Studies. She has been writing about European and American popular and avant-garde film since 1979. Her most recent essays analyze the *Pumping Iron* bodybuilding films, *Tightrope, Fatal Attraction* and 1980s Hollywood sequels and remakes (the Rocky films, *Aliens,* and *Down and Out in Beverly Hills*). She is currently working on a book on Marguerite Duras' experimental cinema.

Alexandra Heidi Karriker is Associate Professor at the University of Oklahoma, teaches courses in Russian language, literature, culture and film. Her essays and reviews have appeared in *World Literature Today* and *The Russian Language Journal*. Dr. Karriker's latest article, "Narrative Shifts and Cyclic Patterns in *Skola dlja durakov*," is forthcoming in *Canadian-American Slavic Studies*. She travels to the Soviet Union frequently and has participated in the AFS/USIA Teacher Exchange Program. She is presently completing a book on the films of Andrei Tarkovsky.

Bruce Murray is an Assistant Professor at the University of Illinois at Chicago; author of *Film and the German Left in the Weimar Republic* (1990); co-author of *Film and Politics in the Weimar Republic* (1982); co-editor of *Concepts of History in German Cinema* (Forthcoming). He has published articles on Weimar film history, New German cinema, and the aesthetic theory of Bertolt Brecht.

153

Wendy Pfeffer is Associate Professor of French at the University of Louisville, where she has taught courses on French culture (high and popular) since 1980. Her primary research interest is the literature of medieval France; she is currently studying the use of proverbs as an example of the mixing of popular and literary traditions in medieval literature.

André J.M. Prévos is Associate Professor of French on the Worthington Scranton Campus of The Pennsylvania State University. He has been teaching French and Spanish courses there since 1983. He holds doctorates from American and French Universities and has published essays on Franco-American relations in French and American journals.

Roger Rollin, William James Lemon Professor of Literature at Clemson University, has been teaching and writing about popular culture since 1970. His most recent essay in this field was on Umberto Eco's novel, *The Name of the Rose*, as a popular culture phenomenon. At Clemson he teaches courses in popular culture as well as in 17th-century British literature, in which area his latest essay is " 'And Laughter Holding Both his Sides': The Comic Milton." He is Vice President of the American Culture Association.

Charles Tatum, Professor of Latin American Literature and Academic Department Head of the Department of Spanish & Portuguese at the University of Arizona, has devoted much of his research over the past ten years to popular culture in Latin America. He is Co-Editor of the journal, *Studies in Latin American Popular Culture*, and Co-Editor of *Handbook of Latin American Popular Culture* (Greenwood Press, 1985). Together with Dr. Harold Hinds of the University of Minnesota, Morris, he is co-authoring a book on the Mexican comic book.

Joan Worley is Assistant Director of Composition at the University of California, Santa Barbara, has presented and published on the film/ literature connection, popular culture, and the use of film in the teaching of writing. She is currently at work on a book on images of disability in American film.

CL

306.
409
04
AME

5001379379